Ophelia's Winter

Ophelia's Winter

By

Sarah Ann Hill

ISBN: 1-58721-681-7

This book should not be used in lieu of professional advice.
The author is not involved in the professional practice of Law or
Estate Planning.

1stBooks – rev. 7/26/00

ABOUT THE BOOK

Ophelia G. McMahon was an American Brown Tabby Kitten who was rescued from the Clearwater, Florida Animal Shelter by retiree Janet McMahon. Miss Janet was diagnosed with cancer and passed away during the "Big Snowstorm of 1993." Ophelia was once again an orphan and ended up in an abusive home. She was confined to a tiny black bedroom for several months, sharing her space with a ball python. The first time Sarah saw Ophelia, she was cowering in a chair beneath a table, hiding from her tormentors. Ophelia looked up at Sarah with her sad green eyes as if to say, "Help me, please."

After an owner's death, many companion animals find themselves abandoned or forgotten. They are given to friends or relatives of the deceased person who may or may not want to care for them. More often, they are surrendered to an animal shelter. Caring for and meeting the needs of a companion animal requires a great deal of individual attention. Every person who owns a pet should be concerned about what will happen to them when we die. As unpleasant as it may seem, this is a problem that needs to be addressed in one's lifetime.

"Ophelia's Winter" explores the plight of abandoned companion animals with enlightening factual material and case histories. Philanthropist Jenny Smith's pets ended up in the very animal shelter she'd established a trust fund for. Benny, Betty and Rambo's owner left a will so detailed that it even included instructions for the disposition of her Seiko watch. What about her beloved companions?

Back in 1946, humorist H. Allen Smith penned the fictional tale of an ex-feral cat named "Rhubarb" who inherited all of his deceased owner's wealth. Unknowingly, this story contained more truth than fiction.

More recently, JFK Jr.'s dog Friday and cat Ruby weren't even mentioned in his Last Will and Testament.

In the end, "Ophelia's Winter" proves to be a "real eye opener" for all pet owners.

TABLE OF CONTENTS

In Memory of:

Janet E. McMahon, C.R.N.A.

1913-1993

ACKNOWLEDGEMENTS

A very special "thanks" to everyone involved in telling Ophelia's story and in the creation of this book.

Jamie Ambrosi-APHIS

Animal Protection Association

Walter J. Cheney-Senior Citizens Site

Jennifer Lea Cohan and Mary Anne Kelly-ASPCA

Merritt Clifton-Animal People

Kevin D. Corbitt-AANA

Custom Business Associates

John J. McGonagle Jr. at Jacat Cattery

Louise N. Naylor, C.R.N.A.

Diana Sharon Nostrand

Donna Pauley and Sylvia Shaffer-KCHA

Nancy Peterson and Julie Shellenberger-HSUS

Jane W. Reily-"CATS" Magazine

Service Office Supply

Ann E. Starcovic, C.R.N.A.

INTRODUCTION-Planning for your cat's care

After a human's death, many companion animals find themselves abandoned or forgotten. They are given to friends or relatives who may not want to care for them, or more often surrendered to an animal shelter. A recent study of independently living elderly people showed that most of the participants assumed a family member or friend would take care of their pet after the owner's death. Caring for and meeting the needs of a companion animal requires a great deal of individual attention. Every person who owns a pet should be concerned about what will happen to them when we die. As unpleasant as it may seem, this is a problem that must be addressed in one's lifetime.

Cats have grown in popularity to the point that they are now the number one companion animal in America. As with that of human beings, the average life span of cats and dogs has increased to the point where you could be looking at making provisions for a pet of 10 or more years.

For a person who becomes ill or injured, most people also do not have someone designated to step in immediately and care for a pet. If the pet owner is elderly or in poor health, the possibility exists that if guardianship became necessary, someone else could end up making decisions about your pet cat.

What things should a cat owner really plan for? Most importantly, someone to take care of your cat/cats in an emergency. Long-term assistance or placement for your cat if you should become indefinitely or permanently incapacitated. Finally, the care of your cat in the event of your own death needs to be addressed.

A growing area of law today in estate planning is the care of one's pet upon the owner's death or incapacity. People are always concerned with passing on wealth to children or other relatives with as little consequences as possible, but what about taking care of a pet?

If you die and your pet survives you, the issue is not going to be just leaving enough money for the pet to be cared for over the long run. Who is going to take care of your pet today and tomorrow?

Courts are reluctant to destroy pets by order of their deceased owners. In contrast to the lovely story of "RHUBARB", who inherited a baseball team, just leaving money to a cat or dog only invites challenges to a will in many states. The courts may convert the bequest to a trust, or invalidate the entire will.

Most state courts refuse to let pet owners establish trusts for the benefit of their own animals, but permit the creation of trusts that benefit the animal population as a whole. There are a few states in which a trust for one's pet may be valid, as long as the amount of money is proportinate to the care needed for the pet after the owner's death.

Without someone to look after a pet's welfare, no amount of money will assure proper care after an owner's death. You can leave your cat to someone, but a cat is considered personal property. It could be treated as if it were a piece of jewelry or an article of clothing. The person could accept your cat, then sell, destroy or just ignore it. That person could also refuse to accept the cat.

While you are still healthy and well, line up a friend or relative whose personality and circumstances are compatible with your cat. Make certain that person is willing to make a commitment to take care of the cat for the rest of its natural life. If such a person does not readily come to mind, make a special effort to find and develop a relationship with such a person.

Animals need human companionship. Pets do not do well over the long-term in isolation or institutionalized settings such as kennels or animal shelters.

Don't just leave your cat/pet to someone without talking to them and feeling comfortable about your decision. You need to make certain that the person is aware of what is involved and is willing to accept the cat.

One of the most common efforts made by owners seeking to protect their cat or dog, is to leave money to a named individual on the condition that they care for the pet. The person can also be left the money and the pet, with your request that the pet be cared for using the money. These types of requests make the most common sense.

Your last will and testament is used to confirm the transfer of your cat to the person who has made a commitment to provide care and to bequeath a gift of money to that person, due to your prior understanding, that will be used for taking care of your cat.

You have to make it clear that the legal custody of the cat has already been transferred by the understanding you had with the person. Under no circumstances do you want the matter of transferring the cat to that individual to become one more time needing to go through the court system.

These types of arrangements can still be challenged even if they seem to accomplish what the owner wants. If challenged, they are generally not allowed.

Do not resort to trusts or conditional gifts without consulting a local attorney who can advise you as to whether your state's laws will recognize or enforce such a device when an animal is the beneficiary. Even if a trust fund is used, a caring and knowledgeable person should be the trustee or oversee the trustee in matters concerning your cat's care.

Another possibility is to arrange for your cat to be placed in a long-term or permanent care no-kill facility. The long-term care facility cares for the cat while working to place it in a permanent home. A permanent no-kill facility will care for the cat.

Most of these types of groups require that you contact them first, so planning for your cat is vital. The Humane Society has argued that your cat may not be happy living in a long-term facility, because many of these facilities take in more pets than they can properly care for.

You should carefully investigate that the organization is committed to and has demonstrated an ability to find a non-institutionalized home for your animal within a very short time after your death. Can they guarantee alternative care immediately after your death, so that not even a day will pass until the cat has the kind of individualized attention it needs? The decision remains up to you.

If you bought your cat from a breeder, some breeders agree to temporarily take cats back, or help place the cat if you can no longer keep it.

Groups which use companion animals may agree to take your cat. However, that may be conditioned on their ability to use the cat, it's age and physical condition.

You may have a few more options if you own a pedigreed cat that has valid registration papers. A pedigreed cat could be considered as having some commercial value. It could mean that whoever handles your affairs must preserve and protect all your assets. The cat would be one.

It would keep the cat from being destroyed, but still would not guarantee humane treatment. However, if you have a pedigreed cat that is a rare breed, you could leave instructions to have a breed group or society contacted by your estate. It could prove useful in finding a new home for your cat.

Whatever option you choose in planning for your cat after your death, or in the event of your incapacity, you have to make certain that your wishes are carried out. You also need to let others know that you have made arrangements for your cat/cats. Advance personal arrangements with a friend or neighbor are also called for. If people who come across your cat after your death do not know what you have planned, they will only do what they think is best.

"Life is life-whether in a cat, or dog or man. There is no difference there between a cat or a man. The idea of difference is a human conception for man's own advantage..."

-Sri Aurobindo (poet & philosopher)

THE HEALING TOUCH

Although she'd retired to Florida to be near her adult niece and nephew, Miss Janet once again found herself searching for love and companionship when she lost Macbeth. He had passed away in Clearwater, leaving her all alone. Macbeth always helped with her checkbook when she sat her desk. Day after day, year after year, he'd shared Miss Janet's innermost thoughts as she recorded them in her diary.

Having focused her career on anesthesiology, she had founded a program where all of her students had lovingly been referred to as, "her girls." Macbeth filled the void in her life. She had never married, instead relying on her pet cat for moral support. Having been a "curmudgeon" by all definitions, she hadn't been surrounded by a large circle of friends.

When the stress of working at the med center got her down, she'd received his unconditional love and support. Macbeth never questioned her decisions or criticized her actions. He had been named after a Shakespearian character with royal ambitions, but Miss Janet's beloved companion had been far more ethical.

Companion animals are family members with whom people share unique bonds. It is often impossible to imagine our lives without them, but they do not live as long as we live sometimes. Just like human beings, pets can suffer from illness, old age and eventually, death.

The death of a companion animal leaves a void in one's life that cannot be filled. Many people feel confused, frightened, angry, guilty and sad. All of these emotions are quite normal under the circumstances.

The loss of a beloved cat or dog can be devastating and the grief may last a long time. Mourning is a highly individual thing. No one can take way the hurt from an individual. It is as natural to grieve the loss of a pet as it is for any loved one who dies. It is also helpful to have compassion and support in your time of grief. Miss Janet did not have that immediate support.

Her friend and colleague Sue had lived nearby during her years at the med center. After her retirement to Florida, Macbeth had been her primary support person.

Annie and Jim had looked upon their elderly aunt's devotion to Macbeth as eccentric. They felt that she'd gone a little overboard in keeping alive an elderly cat who was much like her own self. In the end, their thoughts on the subject had made very little difference to Miss Janet.

Her tears and sadness lasted for a while, until the healing process for her broken heart began to take place. Fortunately for Miss Janet, she had been blessed with a strong need to love and be loved. She didn't take years to reach the stage where she wanted to have another pet in her life. She was determined that she'd find love once again in spite of what anyone said.

It came as no surprise to her when Annie stood in the kitchen, doing her darndest to talk her aunt out of getting another cat.

"Oh Aunt Janet, for pity's sake, you're not getting another cat, are you?"

Miss Janet was an average woman in stature who had shrank a little over the years. Her auburn hair had grayed considerably since her beginning years as founder of the school of anesthesiology, but she still had her father's Irish temper. That never changed. It only meant that Annie would be left standing alone in the kitchen with her mouth wide open as her aunt sped out of the driveway, headed toward the animal shelter.

Resources such as family and friends should always be considered as potential caretakers when an elderly person owns a pet, but one does have to be realistic. Miss Janet was mobile and quite capable of caring for herself, so she hadn't listened to

3

anyone's arguements before driving to the animal shelter that day.

Both Annie and Jim had their own agendas, which consisted of families, jobs and other obligations. There had been little time for watching over their headstrong elderly aunt and soon to be "new pet cat" that would need caring for if anything happened to her. Annie and her family owned dogs that hadn't been socialized with cats, so even the suggestion of introducing a cat into their household had been out of the question.

Annie & Jim also hadn't wanted their aunt Janet to "waste her money". Miss Janet had given them both a copy of her will shortly after retiring to Florida. They were shocked at how well her investments had been doing, so there had been no doubt as to her financial ability of caring for herself and a new pet. It was, after all, her life and her money. She'd made her own and critical decisions for others over the years. She was getting another cat.

Ophelia and Miss Janet first met at the Clearwater Animal Shelter when Ophelia reached out of her cage and touched Miss Janet on the arm with her paw. In that one brief instant, she had stolen Miss Janet's heart. Ophelia, as Miss Janet would later name her, was a magnificent little tigress with an outgoing personality. She had perfect tabby markings from the M on her forehead to the bull's eyes on her sides. Miss Janet had stood by her cage with tears in her eyes, wondering how anyone could have given her up.

According to the most recent national statistics on euthanasia, 76% of the cats entering animal shelters are euthanized. Ophelia had been one of the lucky ones. She'd found Miss Janet.

Macbeth's carrier looked like it was still empty when Miss Janet pulled into the driveway beside the condominium and made her way around to the passenger side of the car. She gently carried her small treasure in the front door using both arms in much the same manner a new mother brings home a baby from the hospital.

Miss Janet had shoved the door open with her foot, so she quickly made a bee line to make certain it was closed, lest her baby escape and fall into harm's way.

Leaving Ophelia in the living room to make herself at home, Miss Janet went into the kitchen where she put out water, kitten chow and a brand new litter pan. Ophelia in the meantime, curiously made her way out of the cat carrier and stretched out in the floor as though it were the first time she'd had enough room to do so. By the time Miss Janet had returned, Ophelia was fast asleep on the oriental rug in the middle of the living room.

Miss Janet awoke early the next morning. She'd always been an early riser, due to her schedule at the hospital over the years. The excitement of having a companion once again had also made her ecstatic. She was thinking back to the days of her childhood, remembering all the fun times she'd had with her kittens. The winters had been colder than cold in Pennsylvania and they'd always had plenty of snow. It had seemed so long ago that she barely remembered the feel of snowflakes flying through the air when she'd made snow angels with her playmates.

"Mow, mow, mow." Ophelia began making her needs known to Miss Janet on their first morning together. She would "mow, mow, mow," until her food was put on the kitchen floor. Miss Janet had laughed loudly at her first words. They were "mow, mow, mow," instead of "meow," like most cats and kittens. Still, there was no mistaking what Ophelia had wanted when the "mow, mow, mowing" began.

Ophelia's time was around 4:00 a.m. She was an early riser like her new mom. They were both morning people, which proved fortunate for kitten and owner. Miss Janet's hours became Ophelia's and vice versa. Cats love routine and order, which Ophelia naturally fell into living with Miss Janet.

Miss Janet and Ophelia both enjoyed the breakfast hour they began spending together each day. They'd while away the early morning hours, discussing the headlines in the daily newspaper over a cup of hot tea and buttered toast. Ophelia always preferred the crust of the bread with just a touch of butter. After finishing her toast, she would proceed to take "nips" out of the edges of the newspaper.

Even though Miss Janet had been brought up in a home where animals were never allowed in the dining room or kitchen areas, Ophelia was always allowed on the table during meals. However, she was only allowed there if they didn't have company.

Non cat owners have such strange ideas about cats, that they never climb up onto the kitchen counter while their humans are sleeping. Annie, Jim and what few visitors there were had proved to be no exception in their perceptions of feline nature. Ophelia's table manners were kept a family secret just between she and Miss Janet.

Ophelia showed Miss Janet over and over how grateful she'd been for her rescue. She gently brushed against her legs at every opportunity, while spending countless hours sitting by her left side in the recliner chair as she read or napped.

She would begin her "mow, mow, mows," if she felt that Miss Janet had been out of the room too long, leaving her by herself. The unconditional love a companion or any other animal has for its owner knows no bounds. It is endless and fulfilling in a way that could never be adequately put on paper.

Ophelia was a ham. She'd chase paper balls across the floor, bat, toss and finally knock them under the sofa. Much to Miss Janet's delight, she even fetched them until she'd tire of the game. Ophelia had catnip mice, fuzzy mice, yarn balls and her infamous catnip sock. She played with it during her nocturnal prowling when no one else was around.

When Ophelia became bored, which wasn't often, she'd venture over to her favorite perch in the window where she'd sniff the salt air and listen to the ocean making its powerful sounds in the distance. Ophelia felt exhilarated as she listened to the waves thrashing against the shore of the nearby beach. Her ears would fold back as she took in the fresh air in much the same fashion as a human enjoying the salty breeze while on vacation.

Although she didn't prefer being on her leash, Ophelia always sat erect in the front seat of the car when she accompanied her Miss Janet. They went everywhere possible together. Loving Ophelia had been very easy and very rewarding to Miss Janet. Theirs was a similar kind of relationship to the one she'd had with Macbeth, but different in other ways. In the case of Ophelia, Miss Janet was retired with more time on her hands living in Florida. If nothing else, it had brought her even closer to Ophelia, who was not as independent as Macbeth had been during all the long shifts she'd spent wotking at the med center.

Miss Janet's life hadn't had much spontaneity when Macbeth was part of her daily routine. Sue, one of her fellow nurses from work had always been her first choice to care for Macbeth if she went out of town. Macbeth had stayed with her and his kitty cousins the time Miss Janet had traveled to England.

Most people who knew Miss Janet were confused by her complete and total involvement in her work, but not Macbeth. She'd been known to be a very private person who only talked about her job.

People who were acquainted with Miss Janet prior to her retirement had felt that she was a very lonely person very much in need of human contact. She often spent hours in the laundry room at the towers, talking with folks who just couldn't seem to get away from her. Some of them took the time to converse with her, while others just went on their way.

Besides her beloved Macbeth, Ophelia had been Miss Janet's only interpersonal contact during the lonely hours after her retirement to Florida. Ophelia loved her Miss Janet with all her heart and Miss Janet loved Ophelia just as much in return. They formed a very special bond.

Miss Janet had also named her after a Shakespearian character. The first day she saw her at the animal shelter, she'd noticed that Ophelia's white eye markings created the illusion that she was wearing little round eyeglasses. It hadn't taken her long to come up with "O"phelia as her name.

Ophelia was often overshadowed by Hamlet in Shakespeare's play, but she was still a deep and interesting character, as was Miss Janet's Ophelia. If one remembers the ending to the story though, Ophelia met her death without her beloved Hamlet by her side.

Perhaps it was a premonition of things to come? Shakespeare, tragedy, people and the sadness they experience in their lives.

Unlike Macbeth, who was an abyssinian cat, Miss Ophelia had been a brown tabby, or American Shorthair cat. American Shorthairs are gentle companions and become wonderful family members. They are known for their good looks, quiet dispositions, good health and amiability with children or dogs.

American Shorthair cats are also known for their longevity, which proved to be a problem in the case of Miss Janet and Ophelia. American Shorthairs are low maintenance cats that can live fifteen to twenty years with just annual veterinary checkups. This meant that given Miss Janet's age at the time she adopted Ophelia, she would have been ninety-five years old had Ophelia lived for twenty years.

Was this a reason to deprive Miss Janet of a companion and condemn her to an even lonlier existence as an elderly retired person? Certainly not!

The financial means for Ophelia's support was more than adequate as long as Miss Janet was alive and even after her death. However, Miss Janet was like the many other independently living elderly people with companion animals. She assumed that one of her friends or family members would see that Ophelia was cared for if anything happened to her. Therefore, she made no provision for Ophelia in the event of her death or incapacity. Ophelia wasn't even mentioned in her "Last Will and Testament", which meant that upon Miss Janet's death, she would become part of the residuary estate. The residuary part of a testator's estate consists of the remaining parts after satisfaction of all debts, charges, allowances, revisions, devices and other bequests have been honored.

A NEW DIMENSION

"She feels it instantly on every side."
The immortality of the Soul, by
Sir John Davies, 1570-1626

Do we deserve the bad breaks that sometimes come in life, in spite of the fact that we've done our best? Of course not, but life is sometimes very unfair.

One of the worst fears for a medical professional, is that you always face the possibility of becoming a patient yourself. A medical professional faced with their own illness has a completely different perspective than any other patient. Experience can offer both advantages and disadvantages when you're told you have cancer.

Being a retired anesthesiologist didn't exempt Miss Janet from any of the initial reactions when given her diagnosis. The past came into focus over and over again. In her dreams, she saw herself standing in the operating room until she'd imagined that she was, in fact, back at the med center.

Since learning to give and receive love is the very fabric of human life, support from the family is extremely important to a cancer patient. Additional support and a greater level of kindness aid in the recovery of a patient. Annie and Jim didn't live with their aunt on a daily basis as did Ophelia. She was Miss Janet's primary support person. They were a family unit.

Companion animals offer a tremendous healing presence and inspiration to their owners. Ophelia drew Miss Janet's attention away from herself and into recovering from her illness. She had sensed her Miss Janet's sudden unhappiness and attempted to dry her tears by rubbing her face against her mom's cheek. She didn't understand cancer, or that there was even a possibility she would eventually loose her rescuer.

During the first few months after her diagnosis, Miss Janet had only been interested in recovering from her illness. Her life had changed since she'd adopted Ophelia from the animal shelter. Ophelia had taught her how to love again after loosing

9

Macbeth. She had something to live for, a friend to talk to, play with and keep her company in what had been a very lonely bed at night. Ophelia hadn't cared if Miss Janet walked around the house all day in her robe or if her hair looked a mess. She loved Miss Janet unconditionally. She would be there until the end.

Miss Janet had never feared anything during her career. She'd always been the healer and teacher to others. Even though she was faced with the threat of death, pain, loss of her bodily functions, abandoned by friends, family and even doctors, she didn't make the most important decision regarding her will. She had no thoughts of what could happen to Ophelia.

Her will had covered lawful debts and funeral expenses to be paid out of her estate after her death. She had directed what was to be done with her remains. She even addressed a list of items of tangible personal property and specified distribution of said items to individuals. Her bequests had ended with the order that advised Annie and Jim to "share and share alike." The one thing that meant the most to her in life had gone unmentioned.

Prior decisions and arrangements were made with her doctor on the course of treatment they would be following. Annie had accompanied her to the admitting office and remained at the hospital until she'd finished her first treatment.

In the meantime, Ophelia was at home lying in her favorite chair, anxiously awaiting the return of her mom. She had nibbled at a little food, but somehow sensed that something was amiss. Mom Janet had left home after taking Ophelia up into her arms for a tearful goodbye hug and many kisses. They hadn't read the morning newspaper or shared their usual tea and toast.

"Mow, mow, mow." Ophelia cried for her Miss Janet from the instant she heard Annie's car pull up into the driveway. When her mom opened the door, Ophelia was crying real little tears. Miss Janet sat down on the sofa and was once again greeted with Ophelia's cheek rubs against her face. Her mom had come home to her, but what were those weird smells? Ophelia inspected Miss Janet from head to foot, not quite understanding what the hospital had done. She finally laid down beside her, as her purrrs grew louder and louder.

Miss Janet put up her small Christmas tree early that year. There were new catnip mice wrapped in tissue paper that Ophelia could easily open. She and Ophelia sat in the soft glow of their tiny tree for hours on Christmas eve. They drifted off to sleep in love and contentment.

RECURRENCE

The word "recur" is defined in the dictionary as, "occurring again after an interval, or turning back in a direction opposite a former course, or to come again to mind."

Recurrence to a cancer patient, means that they have been treated for cancer in the past and that all evidence of the cancer disappeared after treatment. Now, there is evidence that the cancer has come back.

Miss Janet had first hoped for a complete and quick cure to the disease that had begun ravishing her body. Being a medical professional, she had finally settled for a more realistic way of thinking. If her cancer ever recurred, she'd still hoped they could control the disease.

Ophelia and her happiness over the Christmas holidays had helped Miss Janet to forget about her illness temporarily and had raised her spirits more than any medical procedure. Her March checkup brought her right back to where she'd started when she'd first been told of her diagnosis.

For the first time since she'd been living with Miss Janet, Ophelia was unable to console her. She was frightened by her mom's sudden overwhelming tears.

One source of Miss Janet's frustration lay in the limitations of medical science when it came to a cure for cancer. She had devoted her whole life to the healing of others and she'd been informed that the favor hadn't been returned.

A recurrence usually ends up being difficult, because it means that the first attempt at curing the cancer has ultimately failed. Miss Janet decided she was going back to the med center where she'd spent her working years. She wasn't giving up hope.

Against Annie and Jim's wishes, she began making plans to return to the med center where she'd worked for further treatment. She knew that time was of the essence.

There would be no stress involved in making new friends back home in West Virginia. Her own doctor, the residents, nurses and other staff members all knew her. Her friend and colleague Sue was working part-time and would be there to lend moral support.

Miss Janet even phoned the manager at the towers to see if there were any available units she and Ophelia could move into. Macbeth had lived there with her for many years before they'd moved to Clearwater. Janet just knew that Ophelia would love watching the Fourth of July and Labor Day fireworks with her from their special vantage point on the balcony.

All of her records were expressed to the med center on the day she made her decision to move back to West Virginia. Ophelia had a complete folder, which would be going in her suitcase in the car trunk with her jewelry, other important documents and valuables she didn't send in the moving van.

Miss Janet knew it would take several days for the movers to arrive at their destination and had planned her arrival back at her old home place to be "when she and Ophelia got there." They would be on the road for the next five days on what was normally a thirteen-hour drive from Florida. She was determined to return to her roots or die trying.

Miss Janet cried tears of joy when they finally crossed the West Virginia state line five days later. "Look at the mountains Ophelia. Honey look! This is going to be your new home."

She was so overjoyed that she could barely contain herself when they pulled in at the first rest stop they came to. Miss Janet made her way to a pay phone to call her friend Sue. "Sue, Sue, its me! We've made it! We're almost home!"

Her heart pounded as she and Ophelia pulled up to the stop light in front of the med center. "Ophelia! Ophelia! Look honey! There's mom's office. There's the building where mom taught anesthesiology."

Ophelia replied with her "Mow, mow, mowing." She sensed that her Miss Janet was bubbling over with happiness but didn't understand why. All that mattered to Ophelia was how happy her Miss Janet was once again.

They sped away from the light and tore off down the street. Miss Janet didn't slow down until she turned left a short distance from the med center and headed up the hill toward the towers. Sue's car was parked in her old spot, so she wheeled the Ford

14

Taurus in beside it. All she grabbed from the car was Ophelia's carrier. She was moving faster than she had in months as she almost ran across the parking lot and into the lobby of the towers once again. She pushed the elevator button repeatedly until a car arrived to take them up to the fifth floor. They weren't up very high, but that didn't matter. They were home at last.

Sue and Miss Janet both let out screams of glee as the elevator stopped on the fifth floor and Miss Janet emerged with Ophelia in her carrier. Tears flowed until everyone was finally able to contain their emotions. Not understanding all the crying, Ophelia just "Mow, mowed." Her Miss Janet was so happy.

There were packing boxes everywhere, many of which would remain unopened. The furniture had been set up by the moving company, which was all that mattered. Miss Janet and Ophelia could watch television in their favorite recliner chair and once again sleep in their brass bed. They would be comfortable.

The most important thing still remained. That was Miss Janet's Monday morning consultation at the med center. Miss Janet and Opehlia fell asleep on Friday night, completely exhausted from their long trip. She and Ophelia had accomplished quite a task.

Miss Janet awoke the next morning to find Ophelia snuggled against her in the big bed. Ophelia had snuggled closer and closer to her mom with every passing sound from the hallway. She'd recognized the vacuum cleaner, but hadn't understood why it was on the other side of the door.

She finally decided that Ophelia would probably feel a little more at ease if she opened up some cat food and ran her a fresh bowl of water. She'd set up the litter box the night before. Miss Janet then called the building manager's office, confirming that she and Ophelia had arrived. After thanking her for all her assistance, Janet got dressed to take Ophelia out for a drive in her new hometown, which they both enjoyed.

Miss Janet's cheerful mood had once again taken a downturn by Sunday evening. She couldn't even concentrate on television for thoughts of her illness. What were the doctors going to say? Would they be able to help her so she would be there for Ophelia? She turned the set off before her show was half over and retired to bed with Ophelia snuggling next to her. Sue would be coming to pick her up bright and early the next morning.

During her consultation at the med center, the doctors informed Miss Janet that, "they hadn't been able to determine if her recurrence was the same or a new cancer." They comforted her by reminding her there were several good forms of treatment available.

In the meantime, Ophelia had begun exploring her new home in the towers. Miss Janet had carried her out onto the small balcony then brought her back in behind the screen so she could look out at all the mountains.

The smell was completely different from the salty air that Ophelia had found so exhilarating while in Florida. Mountain air was cooler and normally didn't have a faint odor of auto exhaust fumes. However, they were in a city at the bottom of a beautiful valley surrounded by magnificent green hillsides.

While Ophelia was preoccupied with checking out her new surroundings, Miss Janet walked over toward the other side of the apartment where the movers had put her desk and files. She could once again see the med center up the street. Thoughts of all the mornings she'd driven up the street in the rain and snow began to consume her mind. It had been dark on the cold winter mornings when she left on her treks to work. She'd walk from the hospital parking lot and take the elevator up to the employee area. After depositing her personal belongings into her locker, she'd donned her cap and gown. Sometimes she'd been in the classroom, while on other mornings she'd headed for the surgery suites. Her eyes began to well up with tears just as she felt her beloved Ophelia brushing against her legs.

Every day she'd felt the changes that time had been making in the progression of her illness. She didn't want to think of her death or even focus upon a time that she would not be with her loving companion and friend.

MISS NEIGHBORLY AND THE MED CENTER

Ophelia and Miss Janet first met Miss Neighborly one Sunday morning about two weeks after their arrival at the towers. They had just opened up the door and walked out into the hallway to retrieve the newspaper when Miss Neighborly stepped off the elevator. "Hello. Oh, what a beautiful cat! What's its name?"

Miss Janet and Ophelia both looked up at the same moment to see a rather tall, distinguished looking woman. She had white hair that had obviously been put into a curly perm at the salon. "My name is Neighborly, Miss Professor Neighborly." The woman had introduced herself, while at the same time reaching down to pet Ophelia.

Ophelia had lapsed into one of her swooning routines, because she'd recognized the words, "beautiful cat." "You're just absolutely precious." Miss Neighborly had begun stroking Ophelia's back and ego at the same time. Sensing that Miss Neighborly apparently liked cats, Miss Janet proceeded to tell her that "her companion's name was Ophelia."

Being a college English professor, Miss Neighborly had been elated that someone named such a beautiful cat after a Shakespearian character. That in itself had impressed her and everyone who'd ever met Professor Neighborly had known she was quite hard to impress.

Miss Janet had finally met someone who shared her love of the classics, but that had been as far as it went. She and Miss Neighborly were far from soul mates. They had conversations out in the hallway while Miss Neighborly petted Ophelia, but Miss Neighborly's schedule was such that she barely had time for herself. Janet's hours had been much the same during her years as a teacher and administrator at the hospital. You didn't dare get too close to any of the students and there were only a limited number of colleagues who shared a complete interest in the field anesthesiology.

Sue was still around some of the time, but her hours were also limited, due to the fact that she still worked part-time and had a household to run in her off hours. Wednesdays were always the day she and Miss Janet took to go shopping at Foodworld. Ophelia's cat food was the first thing on the list when Miss Janet walked through the electronic doors and immediately aimed her shopping cart down the middle isle with the big "pet foods" sign instead of going the other direction. By that time, she'd started becoming even shorter of breath and had wanted to make certain she'd gotten Ophelia's food before she ran out of energy from pushing the shopping cart.

When Sue and Miss Janet would arrive back at the towers, Ophelia always ran and jumped up onto the little table Janet had stacked in a chair so she could look out the window. She would purr loudly as Sue pet her head. Janet always confided in Sue how "worried she'd become" about who would take care of Ophelia if anything happened to her. Sue had three cats of her own, but Janet had felt that deep down in her heart, Sue would never have let anything happen to Ophelia.

Upon her return to West Virginia, Miss Janet had once again found herself with a very limited circle of friends. She had been gone over five years and many of the people she thought still lived there were either retired like herself or dead. Ophelia was the closest friend she had.

Miss Neighborly proved to be kind in her own way, but she was never there to listen. Ophelia constantly "Mow, mowed" back and forth with her Miss Janet during their frequent long discussions.

Although Miss Janet's general nutrition, digestion and blood counts remained fairly constant, the doctors decided more drastic measures would be needed. They were doing their best. After all, they were treating one of their own.

When the time came for a brief period of hospitalization, Miss Janet knew she would have to rely upon someone to look after her precious Ophelia for a few days. The only person they knew in the towers besides the building manager was Miss Neighborly. Ophelia and Miss Janet waited in the hallway for her the next evening. After inviting her in for a cup of tea, Miss Janet calmly explained the situation and that she needed someone reliable to look in on Ophelia. Miss Neighborly had promised then and there that present or future, she would take care of Ophelia if anything ever happened to Miss Janet unexpectedly. This was a promise Miss Janet relied upon even to her death.

Ophelia ate very little while her Miss Janet was in the hospital. Miss Janet had hugged and kissed her for ever so long before she left, while attempting to explain that she'd return soon. Ophelia only briefly left the living room during her mom's absence for fear that her Miss Janet might return while she wasn't there. She maintained a constant vigil day and night, listening for a key in the door.

Miss Neighborly came over after work each evening and spent time with Ophelia. She'd put out clean food and water, then scoop the litter pan. In her attempts at cheering Ophelia up, she'd turned on the television and sat on the sofa with her until "Jeopardy" went off. Miss Neighborly was company, but she wasn't Ophelia's Miss Janet.

The hospital stay went well and the rest of the chemotherapy sessions were scheduled for an oncologist's office. Back home at last, Miss Janet found that Ophelia had been well cared for by Miss Neighborly. Ophelia once again cried real little kitty tears upon her mom's return. The strange smells from the hospital hadn't made any difference to her. She loved Miss Janet with all her heart and had been lost without her. Annie had looked after her for one overnight stay while they were in Florida. This time it had seemed like an eternity to Ophelia.

Miss Janet had known many people who underwent chemo and later found they could continue their normal activities, but her age had slowed her down. She knew it was going to be longer than just a day or two before she'd bounce back from her hospital stay.

Her Irish temper had gotten her through many of life's challenges. She'd founded the med center's school of anesthesiology back in 1955 during a time when doctors were the aristocracy. She'd been a woman ahead of her time who'd remained strong in the face of adversity. Miss Janet knew how to fight. She'd become determined that she was going to live no matter what it took.

Ophelia sensed that something was terribly wrong, but didn't understand the magnitude of the situation. She remained by her Miss Janet's side twenty-four hours a day. It had made no difference to Ophelia if Janet wore her wig or not. She didn't care if they ate turkey for the holidays or she just had her cat food. Her Miss Janet was the number one priority. She had to be all right.

The smells from all the Thanksgiving turkeys and pies wafting through the elevator shaft at the towers made Miss Janet feel ill. It was one year she and Ophelia weren't sharing their favorite turkey Ophelia had treed behind the glass doors in the oven. Ophelia enjoyed the deli turkey that Miss Janet bought on her shopping trip to Foodworld with Aunt Sue. It hadn't made any difference to her.

Miss Janet decided that she and Ophelia were going to buy a new car when she began feeling better. Maybe they'd even drive back to Clearwater for visit. They knew the way by heart.

Most cancer patients have a circle of friends who respond well to their illness. Friends usually offer to help in any way they can. They help with the shopping, cleaning, driving and other errands. Since Miss Janet's circle of friends had been somewhat limited even prior to her retirement, she and Ophelia became virtually isolated living at the towers.

They'd met Miss Neighborly shortly after returning and had visits in the hallway when she was coming or going. Miss Janet's neice and nephew telephoned from Florida as often as they could. She had her mid-week shopping excursions with Sue. Whenever it became necessary, Miss Janet's transportation to the med center oncologist had also been courtesy of Sue or one of the volunteers. With the exception of Ophelia, she hadn't had much support during the course of her illness. She never revealed how sad she was to anyone but Ophelia.

Miss Janet always had a friend in Sue. When called upon to be her friend, Janet had learned what their friendship had meant to her over the years. Miss Janet had always felt that her relationship with Sue as both a colleague and friend was important to her. Her problem with other people had always been her "insistence upon her individual rights". Friendship involved sharing. Janet had shared more with Sue than she dared with anyone. Their trust grew over the years.

Christmas came all too soon and before Miss Janet had even begun preparations. Annie and Jim had mailed several gifts from Florida and called to check on their aunt. The gifts had only proven to be inadequate substitutes for human warmth and companionship needed in Miss Janet's case.

Sue had called to wish Miss Janet and Ophelia "A Very Merry Christmas!" and to let her dear friend know "she'd be home again as soon as the weather warmed up a little." She and her husband had originally intended to be home for the holidays that year, but ended up in Florida. Miss Neighborly had driven to New England to be with her ailing mother and wasn't even across the hall for their brief visits.

In keeping with tradition, the towers had once again lit the huge star atop the building. It came on every evening at dusk and could be seen all night until after New Year's.

Miss Janet held Ophelia up to the window every night so she could see another big star at the med center up the street. She'd tell Ophelia the story of the star that lead three wise men to Bethlehem, all the while tears were in her eyes as they stood looking toward the place she'd been so dedicated to over the years.

She'd only sent out a handful of Christmas cards that year in response to the few that she and Ophelia had received. A small artificial tree sat on a table near the window with treats for Ophelia tucked beneath its branches. Miss Janet didn't usually enjoy Christmas and had somehow never been able to figure out the precise moment when she'd lost the spirit.

One could say that she didn't want to deal with memories that were too painful for her. Her father was an engineer who had died and been buried in South America while on a job there. One of Miss Janet's most prized possessions was a volume of "The Complete Works of William Shakespeare" that had belonged to her father. It also held a lock of his hair. Her other treasure was an old photograph of her mother and herself taken when she was a young girl. Her father's untimely death and her mother's subsequent remarriage hadn't been easy.

21

As a young girl growing up in a Pennsylvania railroad town during the Great Depression, Miss Janet had realized how much Christmas helped take people's minds off their pain. She'd often wondered "why not hers?" In spite of the loss of her father, she'd still been more fortunate than most. She had a home, food to eat, got an education and had a nice warm bed to sleep in at night.

As the winter sunlight began to fade, she sat in her recliner chair with Ophelia at her side while reading the Christmas cards from Florida over and over. She'd smile when she thought of how proud she'd been of all "her girls" at the med center over the years. Most of the time, she'd found herself so exhausted from her illness that she'd just fallen asleep with Ophelia cuddled next to her. She'd always awakened to the lonely apartment crammed full of unopened packing boxes.

The Christmas story had been on television that Christmas Eve. Miss Janet had sat in her recliner with Ophelia as they watched the portrayal of Mary and Joseph on their journey through the darkness. They saw the mountains of Gilbon where King Saul had died, then the pastures of Dothan where Joseph had once been. Mary and Joseph had finally rested for the night near Jacob's well when evening brought them to the winding road that lead into Samaria.

Miss Janet told Ophelia about all the precious animals that had been in the manger that night. Although she didn't understand, Ophelia realized her Miss Janet was discussing something very important with her.

The next hour had been filled with Christmas carols. Miss Janet smiled at Ophelia when "Let it Snow" was playing. All the singers danced to "Santa Claus is Coming to Town", while Miss Janet recalled her childhood days. "Oh Christmas Tree", "It's Beginning to Look a Lot Like Christmas", and "Deck the Halls" had reminded her of Christmases past at the med center. When the tempo slowed with "I'll Be Home for Christmas", Miss Janet cried the tears that were never seen by anyone but Ophelia. The lonliness finally set in on that dreary Christmas Eve at the towers.

By the time Midnight Mass came on, Miss Janet and Ophelia were both fast asleep. They completely missed the happy sounds of pealing bells and lights sparkling everywhere. Hymns of joy played throughout the disorganized apartment as master and companion slept through it all. Miss Janet's volume of "The Complete Works of Shakespeare" and the picture of her mother sat on a nearby table as she and her beloved Ophelia spent what remained of their last Christmas Eve together.

As her slumber deepened, Miss Janet dreamt about all the events that lead up to Christmas back in Pennsylvania. Millions of people had lost their homes during the Great Depression. There were clothing drives, food drives and fund raising for the poor. It was one's moral obligation to help out. She'd always missed her father, but giving of oneself had been of the utmost importance, especially at that time of year. People were hungry and in desperate need.

Christmas morning 1992 had been crisp and clear down in the valley surrounded by the magnificent West Virginia mountains. The sun shone brightly in a vibrant blue sky that year. There was a sprinkling of snow on the mountaintops, which helped hide the brownish-gray cast that the hillsides take on until spring arrives.

Ophelia and Miss Janet were still asleep in the recliner. They were oblivious to the traffic speeding by on the streets below. People were heading out to visit friends and relatives, or at home opening gifts and enjoying Christmas Day. For Miss Janet and Ophelia, it had been just another day except for the kitty treats she'd wrapped in tissue paper for Ophelia to rip open.

Miss Janet had awakened from her dreams, only to find no one there with her except for Ophelia. She wept as she realized her mother was in an old cemetary with large tombstones behind a black wrought iron fence in Pennsylvania and her father was still buried far, far away.

HER ONLY FRIEND

"All that lives must die,
Passing through nature to eternity."

HAMLET-William Shakespeare
1564-1616

The blizzard of 1993, has been dubbed "The Big One" by the by the NCDC. On March the 12th through the 15th, a storm that is now called the "Storm of the Century" struck on the eastern seaboard. At least 243 deaths were attributed to the storm, plus 48 persons missing at sea. This was three times the combined death toll of the seventy-nine people attributed to hurricanes Hugo and Andrew.

Thousands of people were isolated by record snowfalls. The Virginia mountains, Georgia and North Carolina were hit hard. In North Carolina and the Tennessee mountains, over one-hundred hikers were rescued. Many counties and cities enforced curfews when states of emergency were declared. The National Guard was employed in many of the affected areas.

Every major airport on the east coast was closed by the storm, while hundreds of roofs collapsed from the weight of the heavy wet snow. Three million people were without electrical power due to fallen trees and high winds. At least eighteen homes fell into the sea on Long Island from the pounding surf.

Florida was struck by twenty-seven tornadoes, while twenty-six deaths in Florida were attributed to either the tornadoes or the severe weather. In the Apalachicola area, a nine-foot storm surge was reported. Preliminary damage estimates were as high as one billion dollars. Up to six inches of snow had fallen in the Florida panhandle.

Canada reported three storm deaths in Quebec and one in Ontario. Cuba reported three deaths and Havana had been blacked out. A tornado left five-thousand people homeless in Reynosa, Mexico, which is located near the Texas border.

A spokesman for the National Weather Service's special studies branch said that the volume of water that fell as snow was unprecedented. The NSW office in Asheville, North Carolina reported a snow to water ratio of 4.2 to 1. This had been taken from core samples of new snow. Other core samples taken in nearby areas verified the wet snow with similar results. This equated into 4-5 inches of liquid equivalent precipitation from the storm.

Areas north of Asheville, North Carolina had received dryer snow with similar liquid equivalent amounts. Due to all the weight of the heavy snow, damage to trees and some buildings was extensive. Ninety-nine percent of Polk County, North Carolina was without power during the storm.

The total damage from 1993's "Big One" exceeded one-billion dollars by the time it was over.

During the "Blizzard of 1888", four-hundred people had been killed. Saratoga Springs, New York received fifty inches of snow. Albany, New York had forty-eight inches, while twenty-two inches had fallen in New York City. Snow drifts were over the tops of houses from New York to New England. Eighty mile per hour gusting winds had been a common occurence.

The "1888 Blizzard" was probably more severe in the Northeast and New England, but it had not affected the entire eastern seaboard the way 1993's "Big One" had.

When the snowflakes began falling on the city streets, Ophelia and Miss Janet were at home in their warm apartment. Little did Ophelia realize or even suspect, that she would soon be taken away to the animal shelter in a police car. Her Miss Janet would be gone from her forever. Ophelia hadn't understood why Miss Janet had laid there so cold and still after all her attempts to waken her.

Individuals are all different when it comes to their reactions to cancer drugs. It is impossible to predict who will have difficulty and who will not. A few cancer drugs have very specific effects on the heart or other internal organs. Doctors try to avoid these side effects by regulating the amounts carefully so that the total dose does not exceed the maximum amount that can be tolerated by a patient.

Whether the cause of Miss Janet's death had been chemotherapy or cardiovascular disease, the first few hours after her death were absolute torture for Ophelia. Her Miss Janet had suddenly fallen in the living room floor and Ophelia was incapable of summoning help. She heard the newspaper boy dropping the paper outside the door as he'd always done. The television set kept making the same announcement over and over about "the blizzard headed their way and all the airport closings."

Miss Janet's body had begun turning very pale and she wasn't waking up. "Mow, Mow, Mow." Ophelia softly cried while hoping that Miss Janet would open up her eyes from her nap. She lay on the living room floor beside her that whole first night.

The light coming through the windows early the next morning was very dim and gray, due to the impending snowstorm. Ophelia had felt that her Miss Janet was sleeping late again as she had so often since her illness had returned. "Mow, Mow, Mow" Ophelia had begun getting hungry and whether she'd felt like eating or not, Miss Janet had always seen to it that Ophelia was fed.

By noon, Ophelia heard the cars speeding up and down the streets. Everyone was going to the grocery store to stock up before the storm hit. The light coming in through the windows was still dim and gray. Updates on the weather conditions were still on television.

Miss Janet's body had become quite stiff. Rigor mortis had set in while her mouth and eyes were still open. Ophelia once again attempted to wake her Miss Janet. "Mow, Mow, Mow, Mow, Mow." Ophelia cried even more times and Miss Janet still hadn't opened her eyes or spoken in her kind gentle voice. Ophelia didn't understand. She lay on the floor beside Miss Janet for the second night, curled up against her with her head on her mom's cold chest.

She knew something was terribly wrong with her beloved master. Instead of the soft warm body she'd been accustomed to, Miss Janet was as cold as the snowflakes that had begun falling outside. How could she summon help? Once again, she'd heard the paper boy in the hallway as he made his rounds. She ran over to scratch at the door and cry but alas, he had already gotten back on the elevator.

Miss Janet's body was soft again by the next morning, but her warmth was no longer there. Ophelia was determined to find out why her mom just would not wake up. She'd rubbed and rubbed her face against Miss Janet's, still not getting any response. She very carefully put one paw onto her chest followed by the other paw. Ever so gently, Ophelia sniffed Miss Janet under the nose to see if she was breathing. She positively screamed the loudest she ever had. "MOWWWWWWWWWW!"

Miss Janet's skin was sinking in and pulling away from the tiny bones in her face. There was a smell in the room. It was an awful nasty odor which Ophelia had never smelled before. Miss Janet had died right there in the living room floor. She'd spent her last days with Ophelia and making trips to the lobby of the towers just to pass the time of day with anyone who would talk with her.

The ground outside was covered with snow several feet deep while everything had come to a virtual halt. Ophelia's food and water bowls had been empty for some time as the tv news flashes kept repeating all the closings related to the blizzard.

Once again she lay back down beside her Miss Janet for what would be the last time. Someone knocked on the door then went away. The quiet from the snowstorm had settled in just as Ophelia once again placed her head onto Miss Janet's chest. The stench from her body had filled the whole apartment by that time.

Someone knocked again and again. Ophelia finally heard the manager's pass key turning the lock as she entered the apartment with paramedics and police in tow. By that time, Ophelia was lying on top of Miss Janet's body, whining like a little puppy. She finally realized that her Miss Janet was gone forever.

Since Miss Janet's death had occurred in the apartment, the building manager had to telephone the medical examiner. The police and paramedics didn't move her body until the coroner had arrived to conduct an examination and sign the death certificate.

After the preliminary report had been filled out listing the place of death, date and approximate time, who was with her at the time of her death, her next of kin, their relationship to her, her doctor's name and telephone number, and cause of death, the funeral home was notified to pick up the body.

It had taken several hours before all the necessary formalities had been completed so Miss Janet's body could be removed from the apartment. Ophelia had sat curled up in the corner of the room for a while, then laid down beside her Miss Janet's body once again to protect her from the strangers. She'd been terrified by what was happening.

When the funeral home attendants arrived to pick up the body, one of the paramedics gently moved Ophelia aside as they lowered the gurney and lifted the body from the floor. They had just raised the gurney back to its normal height when Ophelia leapt from the floor up onto Miss Janet's body, wailing loud enough for the whole floor to hear her. "MOWWWWWWWWWWWWWWW!!!!!"

The paramedics stopped in their tracks. One of them broke down crying at Ophelia's demonstrative expression of her grief over Miss Janet's death. Her piteous cries upset everyone in the apartment that day. They had all felt a tug on their heartstrings when they witnessed Ophelia grieving for her beloved Miss Janet. Ophelia had been her best friend and at the last, her only friend.

Miss Janet's will had specified that she be cremated, so the funeral home attendants were on the way to the proper place with the body. The building manager wasn't successful in locating Miss Neighborly and Sue was still in Florida, so Ophelia was taken to the animal shelter via a police cruiser. There had been numerous cat lovers living in the towers who would have been more than willing to take Ophelia temporarily during her time of grief. Instead of taking a minute out to make some inquiries within the building, the manager had instructed the police to deliver her to the local shelter.

Ophelia was dragged from her home in the middle of a snowstorm. She was then placed into the back of a police cruiser with a wire cage isolating her from anyone and whisked away to the same environment from which Miss Janet had rescued her.

The policeman was kind enough to explain to the shelter volunteers that Miss Neighborly would probably be picking Ophelia up as soon as she'd been contacted. It was for that reason alone that she was placed in a separate metal cage and not out in the common cat area. It was cold and drafty with two metal bowls of food and water normally shared by a dozen or so cats.

When a person dies, the loss is usually acknowledged by mourning and or a funeral. The bereaved person is recognized as suffering the loss of companionship and love. With an animal, the feelings of loss and sorrow over a master are usually not shared. Ophelia had been with her Miss Janet only hours before, now she was all alone.

Affection between people and animals is often much deeper than people are willing to admit. As children, we are taught not to reveal our emotions in front of other people. Animals smell our fear and joy because their senses are razor sharp. Ophelia had felt her Miss Janet's despair. Ophelia's grief had been intense in the beginning, then she had lapsed into sadness.

Miss Janet had thought that the cremation arrangements were best for Annie and Jim. They wouldn't have to go through all the details and expenses of a funeral for her. She hadn't wanted to be a burden to anyone before or after her death. Arrangements had been made to accommodate everyone except Ophelia. She had occupied the major role in Miss Janet's life and ended up being discarded as though she'd never existed.

In the meantime, "The Storm of the Century" had struck the city, dumping several feet of snow on the ground. Miss Janet was dead and her body being cremated while Ophelia was locked up in a cage at the animal shelter, abandoned and alone. As she fell asleep on the newspapers in her cage, Ophelia could see her Miss Janet's smile over and over again. Just as she'd begun dreaming that she heard her voice once more, she was awakened by someone calling her name. "Ophelia, Ophelia." It was Miss

Neighborly. The building manager had found her and she'd come to pick up Ophelia.

Ophelia was overjoyed to see a friendly face for a change. Before Miss Janet's death, Miss Neighborly had often visited with them in the hallway. Even though their visits had been brief, they had always been friendly. Miss Neighborly had promised Miss Janet faithfully, "that if anything ever happened, she'd see to it that Ophelia was taken care of."

Miss Neighborly had even brought Ophelia's carrier with a warm blanket to take her home. They immediately checked her out of the animal shelter and headed toward the car for their drive back to the towers.

THE LABYRINTH

According to history, mazes are at least 4,000 years old. During the first 3,000 years, labyrinths consisted of one single convoluted path without any junctions. These were not the puzzles we know today. They were used for ritual walking, running and processions.

The early Romans used the labyrinth motif in their mosiac pavements throughout the Roman Empire. The mosiacs would be the size of a room and square with the image of Minotaur in the center. Minotaur was a monster shaped half like a man and half like a bull. Labyrinthine paths surrounding the monster would make an attractive pattern somewhat like a border.

Labyrinth designs have flourished all over Europe. There are over six-hundred stone labyrinths lining the shores of the Baltic Sea. Many were built by superstitious fishermen who walked through them in hopes of having a good catch and a safe return. Their purpose was also the pursuit of a mate, a courtship, the creation of an embryo with an umbilical cord and birth or new life.

Miss Neighborly had been a bit unaccustomed to sharing her apartment with anyone else. She'd never married or adopted a pet, because those two things would have impeded her spontaniety. She had purchased her cadillac only the previous spring and had put 20,000 miles on it. Since Miss Janet had never been inside Miss neighborly's apartment, she had no idea of the fate to which Ophelia was destined. Miss Neighborly's apartment was a labyrinth.

Ophelia was carried into a labyrinth which was made up of four and five feet tall stacks of books in every direction you chose to look. Miss Neighborly's bed was half full of books, which left a space just large enough for one single human body.

The theme of the movie "Labyrinth" really hit home in regard to Ophelia's relationship with Miss Neighborly. Miss Neighborly had always struggled with the problem of giving up her happy childhood and moving into adulthood over the years. She'd been afraid of loosing everything that had made her happy as a little girl and consequently had never crossed the line. Part of her still lived in a fantasy world. She'd been a Lit major in college, so she still had the chance to play make believe on a daily basis.

Shortly after arriving back at the towers with Ophelia, she'd headed back out again. Luckily for Ophelia, Miss Janet had purchased lots of cat food and litter just before the storm. Miss Neighborly had brought over her blanket, cat bed and soft pillow, carefully placing them in the only available corner of the dining room.

After some exploration, Ophelia finally managed to locate her litter box underneath the bathroom sink. Her food and water had been placed in close proximity to her cat bed, pillow and blanket. It was squeeze, but anything was better than the shelter.

At the time Miss Janet had rescued her as a kitten, 76% of the cats put into shelters were euthanized. Since she'd become an adult cat, her chances of being adopted had decreased even more.

Left alone to wander around her new home, Ophelia decided to use some of her cat logic. Instead of walking through stack after stack of dirty books and sneezing all the way, she decided there was an easier way to navigate the labyrinth. She would hop on top of the stacks and jump from one to the other. That way, she could see down into the apartment and know exactly where she was at any given moment. This would prove to be just one of the problems she'd have with Miss Neighborly. The other one would be her schedule.

When Miss Neighborly returned home that evening, they sat on the sofa while Miss Neighborly read her book in silence. One thing was missing, Miss Neighborly hadn't brushed her like Miss Janet did every evening. Ophelia's brush was no where in sight.

At bedtime, there was also another problem. Where did Miss Neighborly want her to sleep? She and Miss Janet always cuddled together with Ophelia curled up in the bend of her knee. Miss Neighborly was cramped in a fetal position near the books that had been stacked on the other side of the bed. There was no room for Ophelia. She hadn't wanted to go to bed that early anyway, so she decided she'd get in a little playtime in her new home. She knew she'd lost her Miss Janet, but at least she'd been rescued from the shelter again.

Up onto the first stack of books she hopped. Then across to the next row with an even jaunt she went. Hop, Hop, Hop, Hop, her feet thumped along on the stacks of books. All of a sudden, there stood Miss Neighborly in her nightgown. "Ophelia! Ophelia! Bad kitty! Go to bed now!" Clapping her hands in reprimand at a very surprised Ophelia who didn't understand why she was being scolded for playing, Miss Neighborly shuffled her through the stacks of books toward her cat bed.

Once again feeling the pain from the loss of her Miss Janet, Ophelia laid down in her cat bed and fell asleep with her feelings hurt. As her feet began to move back and forth in an animal dream, Ophelia was reliving all the happy times she'd spent with her Miss Janet in Florida. Amidst all the dust from the books, she was imagining that that she could smell the sea air. She was once again sitting in the screen window with her ears flapped back. She saw Miss Janet's smile over and over.

The events of the past twenty-four hours had been so traumatic for Ophelia that she'd gotten completely out of sync. She had no idea what time it was. Miss Neighborly hadn't turned on the television to watch "Jeopardy" or any of the things they'd done when Miss Janet had been in the hospital. In her grief, Ophelia had become disoriented as much as any human being.

She could see the morning light coming through the window. At least it was daybreak. Maybe Miss Neighborly would give her some cat food if she asked?

Making her way through the books without hopping on top of them, Ophelia found her way to Miss Neighborly's bedside where she began her 4:00 a.m. "mow, mow, mowing." She sure didn't get the response she'd gotten from Miss Janet all those years they'd been together.

Miss Neighborly had opened on eye, looked up at Ophelia and immediately gone back to sleep. Ophelia wasn't going to get any food. Thumpa, thumpa, thumpa, off she hopped on top of the labyrinth of books until Miss Neighborly got up five hours later and fed her.

At the time she made the promise to Miss Janet, Miss Neighborly's intentions had been good. She cared about Ophelia. All she had wanted to do, was find a nice person willing to give her a loving home. However, Miss Janet's expectations and Miss Neighborly's good intentions were not in sync. Miss Janet had been an animal lover all her life. She had owned pets and understood their needs. On the other hand, Miss Neighborly had never owned a pet and didn't understand that they come with a lot of responsibility. Ophelia had been like a child to Miss Janet, who had catered to her every whim. When faced with Miss Neighborly's indifference, she felt she was being punished.

Dog people think that introducing a cat into a household is no big deal. You don't have to deal with housebreaking, daily walks and obedience classes. If you are a novice at animal caretaking such as Miss Neighborly, cat hair on the furniture, pawprints all over countertops and kitty games at 3:00 a.m. can get on your nerves. Litterbox training and daily cleanup also take some getting used to.

A new cat owner must also find time for grooming, feeding and interacting with a pet cat. Someone who adopts a kitten or cat from an animal shelter has to find time for socialization and supervision to ensure the cat will become a pleasure to live with.

The fact that Miss Neighborly was a novice cat person, also meant that she'd been a mismatch with Ophelia, who was demanding and used to a routine. She hadn't understood that a commitment to a cat could be as long as 20 years. A cat can add warmth, humor and peace of mind to one's life, as in the case of Miss Janet, or provide too great a challenge as in the case of Miss Neighborly.

When she found that she couldn't tolerate Ophelia any longer, she loaded her into her carrier without even her blanket and drove off up the street to "who knows where". She'd decided the time was right for her to find Ophelia a new home. She couldn't stand the "mow, mowing" any longer.

Bagboy had immediately recognized Miss Neighborly as a regular customer when she walked in to the checkout counter at Foodworld and inquired "if anyone wanted a cat?"

At the time he introduced himself to Miss Neighborly, Bagboy had been working at Foodworld for about a year. Until then, he hadn't been presented with an opportunity to take advantage of yet another innocent victim until Miss Neighborly walked in the door that March afternoon.

The air was still quite chilly from the big snowstorm of the thirteenth. Ophelia could feel the cold wind as Bagboy took her out of her carrier and tucked her under his arm. The feel of his leather jacket somehow made her realize that all she could do was hang her head in sorrow. Miss Neighborly had turned her over to a stranger and hadn't even sent along her carrier with the blanket she'd had since Miss Janet rescued her. She'd been lost without Miss Janet and now there was nothing left from the loving relationship they'd shared for so long. Ophelia just couldn't understand what she'd done wrong to make Miss Neighborly stop loving her.

PROFILE OF AN ABUSER

Neighborhood kids often set cats on fire, torture them or commit other horrendous acts. If they are punished at all, they are only charged with a misdemeanor, even if it ends in death for the cat. Animal cruelty in any form is only a misdemeanor in most states, which means that abusers only receive what is the equivalent to a slap on the wrist.

We devalue cats by allowing them to roam freely. Owners aren't required to register their cats with local animal control or welfare agencies. Cats constantly run the risk of being hit by cars, attacked by other animals and abused by human beings. Today, they are at risk of being shot, burned to death, poisoned or cruelly tortured by sick human beings.

In March of 1997, three teenagers broke into a no-kill animal shelter, where they proceeded to beat 27 cats with baseball bats. Their punishment was 23 days in the county jail. The jury set a value of only $31.25 for the life of each cat that was killed.

A grooming shop in Arizona was broken into by persons unknown. Two cats were tortured in a tub of bleach, one was beaten with a broomstick and they were hung by a noose made from a leash. The abusers had also partied in the shop, turning the radio from a country station to a rap music station.

Many people who witness animal cruelty are afraid to file a complaint for fear the abuser will find out. Others are unaware that there are legal penalties for abusing animals.

There are more theories regarding serial killers than there are actual criminals classified as serial killers. The theory behind who qualifies as a serial killer does provide a pretty good framework. Serial killers are usually white, male and American. They are in their mid twenties to early thirties. Law enforcement courts the definition of a serial killer as a person committing three or more murders and observing a cooling off period between each one.

The serial killer triad consists of three basic behaviors that possibly demonstrate serial behavior into adulthood. These are bed wetting through and after the age of 12, pyromania, or fire setting and animal torture.

Extreme physical, emotional, or sexual abuse from early childhood is frequently traced to most but not all serial killers. The abuse has been perpetrated in the most bizarre and inhumane ways possible. It was suffered from the killer's infancy through teen years.

Questions most frequently asked on a potential serial killer's profile would be: Do you wet the bed? Did you do so after you were 12 years old? Do you enjoy torturing animals? How many cats have you killed? How many neighbors pets have you killed or tortured?

Even if a child is or has been a bedwetter, enjoys torturing animals and setting fires to things, it still doesn't mean that they will end up being a serial killer. It just means that it is likely.

Author Stephen King wrote a book he called "It". He told the story of a little boy named Patrick who liked to lock animals in an abandoned refrigerator until they died from asphyxiation. An evil monster got Patrick before he'd been able to work his way up to another person.

There is a long list of serial killers who practiced animal torture before they went on to murder other human beings.

Michael Cartier threw a kitten through a closed window when was only four years old. He also pulled a rabbit's legs out of its sockets. Cartier shot Kristin Lardner in the head three times. She later died from her wounds.

Henry Lee Lucas killed animals and then had sex with their corpses. He killed his mother, his common law wife and an unknown number of people.

Edward Kemperer cut up two cats. He killed his grandparents, his mother and seven other women.

Theodore Robert (Ted) Bundy witnessed animal cruelty committed by his grandfather. Ted Bundy went on to kill thirty-three women.

Jeffrey Dahmer participated in the deliberate killings of animals by car. He then murdered 17 men.

Richard Allen Davis, the murderer of little Polly Klaas, set cats on fire.

Serial killer Randy Roth once taped a cat to a car's engine and used an industrial sander on a frog. He later killed two or his wives and attempted to kill a third.

Albert De Salvo, known as The Boston Strangler, would place a dog and a cat in a crate with a partition between them. After starving the animals for several days, he would remove the partition and watch them kill each other. De Salvo raped and killed nine women by strangulation. He often posed the bodies in a shocking manner after death.

Richard William Leonard's grandmother forced him to kill and mutilate cats and kittens when he was a child. Leonard killed Stephen Dempsey with a bow and arrow. He killed Ezzedine Bahmad by slashing his throat. He finally shot and killed five men.

Eric Smith strangled a neighbor's siamese cat at the age of nine. At the age of a thirteen, Smith bludgeoned Derrick Robie age four to death. Smith lured the younger boy into the woods, choked him, sodomized him with a stick, then beat him to death with a rock.

Arthur Shawcross repeatedly threw a kitten into a lake until the kitten drowned from exhaustion. He killed a young girl. After serving 15 1/2 years in prison, he was released and killed 11 more women.

When 15-year old Kip Kinkel opened fire on his Springfield, Oregon classmates killing one and injuring 23 others, it was not the first time he had killed. Kinkel had been known for cutting off the heads of cats and mounting them on sticks.

Violence in our society is disturbingly common today. The news abounds with horror stories like these which involve acts of cruelty to both animals and people. Recent studies involving the anatomy of cruelty show a clear connection between acts of animal cruelty and crimes against human beings.

The FBI began to see a connection between cruelty to animals and other violent behavior in the late 1970's. They conducted a study of serial killers and found that most had either killed or tortured animals as children or adolescents. The FBI's study reported that animal cruelty is not a "harmless venting of emotion" in a healthy individual, but a warning sign that the individual needs some sort of intervention.

Even though the link between cruelty to animals and other forms of violent behavior has been well documented, it hasn't been taken seriously by law enforcement officials, social service agencies and the courts. Animals are treated as property, so crimes against them are only misdemeanors. State anti-cruelty laws are weak and inadequately enforced. Twenty-one states now have felony animal cruelty statutes on the books. A new law in California requires psychiatric counseling for offenders.

There are many more killers who started abusing animals and finally progressed to human beings. Federal legislators recently found it necessary to spend a weekend learning how to be more civil to one another. Dozens of mature, educated people needed to learn how to treat each other with courtesy and respect.

Is it any wonder then, that we learn of so much disrespect for animals and their well being? Today's animal abusers are tomorrow's child abusers and serial killers. Humane Education will be the only solution to any long term success in wiping out the problem.

Humane Education is all about kindness and respect. By encouraging the value of all living things, humane education fosters an appreciation of the environment and all creatures in their respective habitats. It also teaches people how to accept and fulfill their responsibilities to companion animals and to understand the consequences of irresponsible behavior. Humane Education also encourages people to find out more about animals and their roles in the environment through non-invasive, observational methods.

Effective Human Education efforts require the use of ideas and programs that interest students and encourage interaction with classmates, which promotes critical thinking, evaluation and decision making. Children can become frustrated when they are unable to solve a problem or have little or no control over a situation. If an issue is raised, it is crucial that options and opportunities are provided that children can pursue.

A child should be taught to interact appropriately with pets from the moment they begin to move around on their own. Children investigate everything around them, including pets, pet toys, water bowls and the cat litter box. Young children have no conception of the pain they inflict by biting, stepping on, jumping on, kicking, hitting, or pulling on a pet's body. Children may also take delight in waking a sleeping pet by screaming in its ear, chasing it, or giving it no peace.

Children must be taught how to treat pets. They must learn that pets are not toys. They are living beings and also feel pain. Children must also be shown which part's of a pet's body can be touched and how to pet them. They need to be taught not to disturb a pet while it is sleeping, eating, or playing with a favorite toy. Children need to be taught not to pursue a pet that runs away and not to restrain a pet that is attempting to break free. Children must understand their own physical strength and the consequences of their behavior.

If a child is uncooperative, it is necessary to keep the pet and child separated until the child demonstrates more self-control. Sometimes, it can become necessary and even humane, that a pet be placed into another home. The most reliable and tolerant animals have a breaking point. Sometimes children and pets are not a good mix and you are better off waiting until children are old enough to demonstrate consistent responsible behavior before bringing pets into your home. A child who exhibits extreme and repeated cruelty toward animals is most likely in need of professional counseling.

Given the increasing violence that children are subjected to in today's world, The American Society for the Prevention of Cruelty to Animals, or ASPCA, offers a variety of educational materials for use by parents and teachers to help children learn respect for all living things.

Teaching children humane education has been part of the ASPCA'S programs since 1916. The ASPCA'S first humane education program was launched with the creation of educational materials that were distributed to schools throughout the New York area. Today, the ASPCA incorporates humane education with entertaining information as an essential part of school programs and activities nationwide. The ASPCA Humane Education Department had distributed classroom materials to approximately 20,000 schools and teachers across the country.

Saint Francis of Assisi was known as one of the greatest Christian Saints of all time. He is also remembered as someone who "talked to the animals". He has been called "A Mirror of Perfection" who's example was followed by many other saints. His message is still used to promote peace in the world today.

His tradition of Blessing the Animals has gone on for many generations. Varities of animals attend this tradition including chickens, donkeys, rabbits, birds, dogs and cats. Many nonprofit organizations dedicated to teaching children about respecting nature are also frequently in attendance at Animal Blessings.

Although Ophelia's new owner hadn't officially been declared a serial killer as such, his behavior patterns fit into the triad of recognition used to identify such an individual. He had been a bedwetter through high school and he'd also enjoyed torturing animals. He'd been caught with a cassette taped episode of an actual torture session involving his pet guinea pig. While sticking lit matches to the fur on the guinea pig's sides, Bagboy had delighted in hearing its agonizing screams. He'd taped the whole session so he could listen to the innocent little animal in pain over and over again.

After exhibiting disrespectful and anti-social behavior toward teachers and other students at school, he'd been transferred to classes for behavior disoriented students.

After graduation, Bagboy had been unable to keep a steady job. His longest tenure of employment had been bagging groceries and stocking at Foodworld. Given his profile, what chance did Ophelia have of making it out alive and unharmed? The odds were slim to none.

BAGBOY AND THE BALL PYTHON

Ball pythons are found on the edges of the forest lands located in Central and West Africa. They are comfortable living in the trees or on the ground. Ball pythons are particularly active around dawn and dusk. This would make them somewhat similar to a cat in their prowling habits. They are called "Balls" in the United States because they curl themselves up into a tight ball when they are nervous. Ball pythons are by nature, curious and gentle snakes.

By adulthood, ball pythons can reach four feet in length, although there are occasionally those snakes reaching five feet in length. Boa constrictors and ball pythons both have anal spurs. These so-called claws, are the remains of hind legs that the snakes lost during evolution from lizard to snake millions of years ago. Male ball pythons have longer spurs than females.

Pythons and boa constrictors are known to devour birds, small mammals, lizards and even other snakes. Ball pythons tend to be picky eaters and are reputed to be able to go for extended periods of time without food.

Ball pythons are killed for food in Africa and their skin is used for leather. With the increased popularity of reptiles as pets, more than 60,000 ball pythons are imported annually. Ball pythons harbor several different types of parasites which can go unnoticed to an inexperienced snake owner.

These snakes grow about a foot a year during their first three years of captivity. Most of them reach sexual maturity in three to five years.

Bagboy's pet python was living in a glass tank with screen wire on top. He used a rock from the yard with which to keep the small sheet of screen wire in place whenever he wasn't in his bedroom. What he didn't know, was that ball pythons are very cunning and powerful when it comes to escaping from their cages. What an ignorant and incompetent snake owner didn't know, had therefore put Ophelia in grave danger in her new home.

The bedroom in which Ophelia was imprisoned with the ball python had been painted black. There was a small round table with two chairs in one corner, while the snake's tank had been placed on a stand at the other side of the room.

Mr. and Mrs. B. were standing by the door when the car with Bagboy and Ophelia pulled up. "What's that you have under your arm?" Mrs. B. had inquired as Bagboy came up the walk carrying a forlorn looking Ophelia. She had obviously recognized that it was a cat but had wanted to make conversation with her son before he adjourned to the bedroom. Bagboy had been born to Mr. and Mrs. B. later in life. Many people who knew him had considered him to be a spoiled child who's parents had indulged his every whim and "let him get away with murder", so to speak.

Bagboy didn't stop for idle chatter with Mrs. B. as he proceeded down the hall and kicked open the bedroom door. Ophelia was overwhelmed at the darkened room which held very strange smells.

Walking back toward the door, Bagboy reached for a switch and turned on a dim light under which Ophelia could see the objects in the room, including the strange looking glass case perched atop its stand. Her new owner then went into the kitchen to eat supper before putting down her food, water or even a makeshift litter pan. Sitting in the dimly lit room, she could overhear him conversing with other individuals out in the kitchen. It had been over twenty-four hours since she'd eaten and had a drink of water. Ophelia was hungry and thirsty, but she somehow knew that "mow, mowing" to make her needs known wasn't going to do any good.

When Bagboy reappeared, she was waiting for him at the door. Maybe he'd fix her something to eat and they could cuddle up on the bed for a nap. She was instead greeted with an exhibition of behavior she'd never even had in nightmares. "Ah! Ha! Ha! Ha! The devil's got you now!"

Terrified, Ophelia spun toward the bed in one quick leap. That did not save her from Bagboy. His pursuit of her began as he once again repeated his initial threatening tirades of "Ah! Ha!

Ha! Ha!, Ah! Ha! Ha! Ha!" Bagboy proceeded to pursue a now hysterical Ophelia around the tiny bedroom.

When Bagboy finally cornered her, Ophelia only saw one way out. She jumped onto the drapes and with her long sharp claws, pulled herself all the way to the rod near the ceiling. Her heart pounded and her pupils dialated as she hung on for her life, hoping that Bagboy didn't yank her down.

Ophelia's Miss Janet must have been watching over her. Bagboy had apparently gotten his entertainment for the evening. After laughing at her repeatedly, he flipped on a small portable television set which stayed on through the rest of the night.

Once Ophelia heard his snores, she knew it was safe to come down from the drapery rod. She very, very quietly slinked past the bed toward the small round table where she climbed up into one of the brown chairs. She didn't sleep the whole night. As she was curling herself into a ball, she suddenly discovered that she'd peed all over her hind quarters.

Morning came and Bagboy was once again off to work at Foodworld. Ophelia had known better than to even attempt her 4:00 a.m. "mow, mowing", asking to be fed.

Once her tormentor was gone, she received a wonderful surprise. Mrs. B. Opened up the door to the torture chamber allowing her to roam free in the house. She found fresh cat food and water out in the kitchen, where old Mr. B. petted her. He told Ophelia how pretty she was. Old Mr. B. reminded her of her Miss Janet in a lot of ways.

Ophelia spent a long time sitting beside Old Mr. B. on the living room sofa. It had been almost like having her Miss Janet back. Old Mr. B. had stroked and petted her in much the same manner, while talking to her about everyday matters.

When Old Mr. B. settled in for a nap. Ophelia set about exploring the rest of the house. The sun was shining brightly into a room directly across the hall from the torture chamber, so she decided to take a peek inside. It was another bedroom with a huge bed covered in quilts and soft pillows.

Ophelia felt so relaxed as she settled in between the pillows for a warm afternoon nap. She slept and slept and slept, all the while dreaming of her Miss Janet once again. "Why had her Miss Janet left her all alone? Oh Why?"

She was abruptly awakened when Bagboy returned home from work once again. It was evening and the dim shadows had fallen into the room where she'd found comfort from all the trauma she'd been through. Not only would she be enduring torment from Bagboy that evening, the two apprentice torture nephews were coming over to see Bagboy's new cat.

KJ and JJ as they were called, were exact carbon copies of Bagboy in every sense of the word. The first thing they did, was to chase Ophelia up the drapes once again with a "hisssssing" sound. Bagboy and the torture nephews had stood cackling as they watched Ophelia cling to the drapes in terror. She was once again being subjected to the previous night's atrocities except that she now had three tormentors in lieu of one. KJ asked Bagboy if Ophelia had figured out there was a snake in the room yet? He had laughingly replied, "Not yet, but wait til she does. She'll live on top of the drapery rod."

With more cackling and laughing, they had adjourned to the kitchen where Mrs. B. was making frozen pizzas. Nothing was said as to the commotion that had previously been overheard coming from the torture chamber. Nothing had ever been said regarding anything that had gone on in the black bedroom. It was the devil's own private domain.

Ophelia had already cowered into the brown chair underneath the table by the time Bagboy came to bed. KJ and JJ had gone home for the evening after they'd finished playing computer games.

When Ophelia heard Bagboy's snorning once again, she very quietly hopped down from the chair. Making every effort not to disturb him, she slowly crawled toward the door underneath which she could see a light. With her very softest "mow, mow, mow, mowing", she began scratching the bottom of the hardwood door that separated her from the rest of the house. Long into the wee hours of the morning she figured out that her efforts had all been in vain. She was doomed to be spending her nights in Bagboy's torture chamber.

With the coming of daylight once again, Bagboy left for work and she was set free. She flew out into the kitchen to get a bite of breakfast then ran into the bathroom to use the litter box before joining old Mr. B. on the sofa.

Her afternoon was spent in the warm sunlight streaming through the glass window panes while she slept. She was awakened again when Bagboy came home that evening.

A few days later, Ophelia made a terrifying discovery. She had company in the torture chamber, company that no self respecting, or for that matter, no cat needed.

A strange odor had permeated the black bedroom from the first day Bagboy had brought Ophelia home. Ophelia knew that she was free to roam the house during the day and be fairly safe in doing so. One afternoon, she finally decided to explore the torture chamber and see if she could locate the source of the strange odor.

She'd observed the strange glass tank sitting in a corner opposite the table where she cowered to avoid being tormented. Having never been around reptiles, the glass tank was completely unfamiliar to Ophelia. She'd met birds when she and Miss Janet had gone visiting in Florida, but never any snakes.

As she slinked back into the torture chamber that afternoon, she noticed that the peculiar smell had gotten stronger when she turned her nose toward the glass tank containing the python. Ophelia cautiously moved toward the snake's tank in hopes of getting a look at the mysterious creature. Just as she braced her front paws up onto the front of the metal stand, the python moved. Suddenly scared out of her wits, Ophelia fled across the hall to the other bedroom. With her heart nearly pounding out of her chest, she ran underneath the bed and curled up into the corner where she remained until evening.

Ophelia was not only being tortured, she was also in danger of being crushed to death in the snake's coils as she suffered a painfully slow, agonizing death. Since pythons were master escape artists, Ophelia could have been crushed to death with Bagboy in the same room snoring. No one would have heard her cry with a python wrapped around her in the brown chair.

Ophelia's reaction to being locked in the black bedroom once again had tipped off Bagboy that she'd finally made the fatal discovery. She was more than aware of her reptile companion residing in the glass tank. Therefore, he decided that it was feeding time for the snake. He would make Ophelia watch him feed the snake a live mouse.

Bagboy yanked the brown chair out from under the table and proceeded to toss Ophelia up onto the bed by the scruff of her neck. Daring her to move, he went over to the glass tank and lifted the rock from the screen wire. It had been a miracle that the snake hadn't escaped. As Bagboy reached down into the tank to bring the python out, it suddenly "bit him" with one quick thrust of its head. "Ah! Ha! Ha! Ha! so you choose to bite me do you?" Bagboy drew back his hand with blood very visibly dripping from two puncture marks near his thumb. The python had begun lashing its tail and hissing. Even the snake didn't like being handled by Bagboy. Apparently there was no level of trust and confidence with the snake either.

Since Bagboy had been determined to torture Ophelia, he lifted the python from the tank anyway. "Moooooooooooowww-wwww!!!!" Ophelia screamed in terror as Bagboy carried the snake toward her. Up the drapes she went with claws bared to escape the worst terror she'd ever experienced. "Why oh why had her Miss Janet gone away and left her?"

As if the snake and Bagboy's constant tormenting hadn't been enough, Ophelia had begun to itch. She scratched day and night until she'd nearly rubbed herself raw behind the ears. Miss Janet had always been extra careful upon entering and exiting the condo in Florida. She'd always told Ophelia "that there were fleas in the grass." Ophelia had no idea what fleas were, that is, until the started living with Bagboy. The carpet in the black bedroom was infested. Ophelia became even more miserable from the plague she'd been thrown into. There had been no escaping the tiny hopping creatures as they went from the carpet to the beds, then onto her.

Most serial killers, or those who fit the triad, sooner or later take a break. Many are known to cease their activities for a month or more before murdering another victim.

Bagboy and the nephews were tiring of their evening routine of chasing Ophelia up the drapes and laughing hysterically when she peed herself. It was time to search for a new victim. Bagboy decided that he'd put an ad in the paper. Maybe he could trade her to someone for another snake. His classified went as follows:

> CAT! WILL TRADE FOR SNAKE OR MONEY.
> DON'T WANT ANY MORE!
> PLEASE CALL 555-BAG

ONE BLESSED CAT

I was browsing through the Sunday morning paper early in June when I came upon the strangest classified ad I'd ever read:

"CAT! WILL TRADE FOR SNAKE OR MONEY.
DON'T WANT ANY MORE.
CALL 555-BAG"

My initial response had been to laugh out loud. I'd thought the ad was the funniest thing I'd ever read. Having worked in the newspaper business while attending college, I had met some of the strangest people in the universe coming in to place all sorts of ads. All at once, my heart nearly stopped. I sat there frozen. "Oh my God! It wasn't a joke. Some poor innocent cat needed help and fast." I'd never been on a rescue mission per say, but I had become educated on the plight of cats and all abandoned animals through the adoption of Schnookums. Schnookums had been found all alone on a MacDonald's parking lot as a tiny kitten.

With the Sunday classified section still in my hand, I sat my coffee cup down on the table and picked up the phone. My hand trembled as I dialed, "555-BAG". To my surprise, an an older woman's voice answered the phone. "Hello, hello." I caught my breath for a second time then spoke to the woman's voice on the other end of the line. "I'm calling about the ad you have in the newspaper. I don't have any snakes, but I'll be glad to pay you for the cat."

The woman's voice sounded calm as she said, "well, its my son's cat, but I know he'll be glad to sell or maybe even give it to you. Do you have a cat carrier? Bring it with you."

My own nervousness became very apparent during the next thirty minutes or so, as I flew up the interstate then turned off onto a rural secondary road leading to the outskirts of the city. After slowing down and scanning mail box after mail box, I saw the "BAGS". I had just passed it and had to back up, finally coming to a screeching halt directly in front of their house. I didn't even take time to bring the cat carrier in from the front seat.

Bagboy and Mrs. B. had been watching for me through the front window when I pulled up. "I'm glad you came. I'd been running that ad for several days with no replies. Guess nobody wants and old cat these days." Bagboy finished his speech while motioning me toward the back bedroom at the same time.

The first time I saw Ophelia, she had been confined to the tiny bedroom for several months and was cowering in a chair beneath a table, hiding from her tormentors. She had been in a daze since the death of her beloved Miss Janet, bewildered and at the mercy of the world. As I walked into the room that day, Ophelia looked up at her with her sad green eyes as if to say, "Help me, please." There was no way I was going to leave without her.

Ophelia was the most beautiful cat I'd ever lain eyes on.

I Immediately fell in love with her. Ophelia didn't deserve what she'd been through. Miss Janet had unknowingly relied upon a promise from a neighbor that, "she would find a place for Ophelia after her death." Ophelia had almost gone to her own death as a result of that promise.

While gently reaching down and scooping Ophelia up into my arms, I told Bagboy to bring in the cat carrier from the car. After I'd safely secured Ophelia inside and latched the door, Mrs. B. came in to say good-bye. "Ophelia, this lady is going to be your new mom." She smiled as she stuck her fingers into the cat carrier and scratched Ophelia on the head one last time.

Bagboy had to get in one final taunt as I was headed down the front walk with Ophelia. "Ah! Ha! Ha! You know the devil don't you?"

I had felt like hitting him, but instead opted to get Ophelia out of harm's way as soon as possible. She and I sped off down the highway, never to return.

A traumatic experience can shake the foundation of one's beliefs about safety and shatter any assumptions about trust. Because traumatic events are so far outside what we normally expect, they provoke reactions that seem strange and crazy. No matter how unusual and or disturbing a reaction to trauma is, it is typical and expected. These are normal responses to abnormal event's in one's life. These facts apply equally to animals as well as human beings.

I had guessed that Ophelia had been through quite an ordeal just from seeing the black bedroom with snagged rapes and a snake tank in the corner. I knew that if Ophelia were to recover, it would have to be with lots of kindness and understanding.

Since most cats do not readily accept a stranger, I had no idea how Schnookums and Ophelia would react to one another. Not wanting to chance a cat fight after what Ophelia had been through, I fashioned a temporary petition out of two window screens and a roll of duct tape before releasing Ophelia from the cat carrier. I then put Schnookums in the bedroom doorway on one size of the makeshift contraption. She would have a bedroom and a home office to roam in, while Ophelia could prowl the living room, dining area and kitchen.

In the ideal world, a new cat introduced into a home should be younger and smaller than the existing cat. The new cat should also be a sexually immature (kitten) or a spayed/neutered member of the opposite sex.

The reality of the situation with Ophelia, was that there had been no other choice. Finding a stray on the street, falling in love at a shelter, or rescuing a victim like Ophelia is one of those events. Spouses and lovers with pet cats often come as a "package deal" that is non-negotiable. This kind of introduction can be rough on all concerned. I had initially tried to prevent this occurence.

Ophelia had been larger than the existing cat, Schnookums, but they were only a couple of years apart in age. Schnookums and Ophelia were both neutered females with similar temperments. Ophelia was an amiable American Brown Tabby while Schnookums was a blue mixed breed, bearing a hint of tabby striping on her tail. They had both been pampered by their respective moms as kittens and young adults.

Ophelia had seemed very shy and afraid of intimate contact at first, so I just left the room to spend some time with Schnookums so she could take her time exiting the cat carrier. I later noticed that Ophelia had fleas, but decided to just observe her for a while since Schnookums was taking a nap.

Miss Ophelia slowly made her way over to the partition, then went into the kitchen for a drink of water. I had set up a temporary litter box, in addition to the food and water.

When Schnookums awoke from her nap, Ophelia was standing at the screen checking out the situation. They both "hissssssed" a little at first sight. Without any intervention from me, both cats finally calmed down and just stood on each side of the little fence looking at one another. I immediately took it as an indication they'd probably get along. Schnookums had been a prima dona, but so had Ophelia whenever she'd lived with Miss Janet. I chuckled at the fact that the two prima donas seemed to appear compatible.

Realizing that I had to do something to prevent Ophelia's fleas from infesting the carpets, I pulled several large bath towels from the closet and ran a bucket of warm water in the bathroom tub. After grabbing a flea comb from the closet, I sat Ophelia in the bath tub on one of the big fluffy towels and gently combed her fleas while drowning them in the bucket of water.

I gently spoke to her and assured her that "everything was going to be all right" as I slowly ran the flea comb through her coat and swished it into the water time and time again.

I sat with Miss Ophelia for over an hour before finally drying her off as best I could with one of the fluffy towels. Ophelia was then given free reign of her half of the apartment so she could explore her surroundings.

Unknowingly, I had provided Ophelia with something familiar and in which she found comfort. There were several U-Haul boxes full of files sitting in the home office. Who would have ever thought an accountant's boxes of papers would mean so much to a poor kitty? At the time, I knew nothing of Ophelia's past and that her previous home had been partially furnished with U-Haul boxes that had never been unpacked from Miss Janet's move.

The next morning, I found Ophelia sound asleep on one of the U-Haul boxes. She was as relaxed as though she'd always lived with me.

The veterinarian I used for Schnookums felt as sternly as I did about animal cruelty and examined Ophelia from head to paw. Had she found any evidence of torture, I had intended to bring charges against Bagboy. Luckily, Ophelia was physically all right except for a few remaining fleas I had missed the previous evening.

Although I didn't know what the outcome would be, I removed the temporary partition the next evening. I gritted my teeth as I slowly peeled off the duct tape and removed the barrier between my two pet cats, all the while hoping for the best.

After a brief round of mutual hissing from both cats, Schnookums first "sniffed Ophelia's butt". Determined not to be outdone by her new housemate, Ophelia in turn "smelled Schnookums' butt". They went their separate ways. The introduction hadn't gone so badly after all.

The following evening, I came in from work to find them sharing the bed together. Schnookums was at the head and Ophelia was sleeping soundly at the foot. They were going to be friends.

Post-traumatic stress disorder is most often talked about as a condition affecting human beings. It is a term most commonly used to describe symptoms arising from emotionally traumatic experiences. A human being who has experienced a traumatic event involving actual or threatened death and or injury to themselves is affected by post-traumatic stress. That person feels fear, helplessness or horror. The three main symptoms in post-traumatic stress are what is termed intrusions, or flashbacks and nightmares, avoidance when the victim tries to reduce exposure to people or things that might bring on intrusive symptoms or hyperarousal. Hyperarousal means physiologic signs of increased hyperarousal, such as hypervigilance or "startled response".

Cats also experience stress, which is not that different from human beings. Many of the same situations that upset people, also upset cats. Intrusive neighbors, uninvited guests, unfamiliar places, noises, smells and changes in diet can send cats into "stress-induced anxiety".

Another similarity between feline and human stress, is that each cat has an individual tolerance for change and stress. It could take moving into a new house to upset some cats and something like getting a new sofa for others. Cats are just like people, in that they are most comfortable when they are familiar with their surroundings.

Getting a divorce, loosing one's job, a family move or a death in the family are all stressful events in anyone's life, animal or human. Ophelia had lost her Miss Janet and been taken to the animal shelter in a blizzard. She'd been picked up by Miss Neighborly and had been forced to live in a labyrinth for several days before being stripped of all her earthly possessions, down to her carrier. After being handed over to Bagboy on a supermarket parking lot in the cold, she'd been imprisoned and tortured for several months. It was a miracle that she'd remained alive.

What may appear to be a quiet, reserved type house cat, could actually be an animal going through mental anxiety and metabolic degeneration. There are many different outward appearances of stress. The stereotypical picture of someone bouncing off the walls is often not the person really undergoing stress in their lives. Stress gradually causes physical exhaustion, impairs mental function and brings about metabolic changes within our bodies.

Cats show stress in fairly subtle ways that we can sometimes pass off as "behavior". While imprisoned in the small bedroom, Ophelia had taken to spending the majority of her time lying in a chair underneath a wooden table. She hadn't even reacted to my invasiveness when I first picked her up out of the chair during her rescue.

Cats were originally meant to be solitary animals that fended for themselves and only associated with other cats for breeding. People have created an environment that is very different for them. Cats live with humans, other pets, hear strange noises and are often restricted in space.

Changes in a cat's behavior can also directly affect their health. A cat that spends the day hiding, such as Ophelia had, or lying around is more likely to develop problems related to lower water intake. Older cats may develop kidney failure, or Feline Urologic Syndrome. Constipation can also become a problem. The cat can even loose weight, since getting to the food dish means taking a risk. In the end, the cat's coat and skin become matted and flaky, because the cat needs to feel comfortable and secure to think about self grooming.

Ophelia's stress level had not been at the top of anyone's list until she met me. Shortly after being rescued, she had still exhibited symptoms of post-traumatic stress. If I walked up behind her unexpectedly, she'd lapsed into a tyrade of formidable "hissssssing." Ophelia had nightmares while sleeping, during which her paws moved, galloping as if in a running motion. She'd suddenly awaken "Mow, Mowing," while seeming not to know where she was. She was frightened by the slightest unexpected sound.

After about a month, it became apparent to me that Ophelia and I had developed an element of trust. Ophelia's sudden hissing had greatly decreased and she'd begun spending the night tucked in bed against the back of my knees.

Ophelia sat beside me on the left sofa cushion when I watched television with Schnookums lying behind us. Her purrrs could be heard throughout the room when I brushed her.

I really knew Ophelia had made herself at home the evening I caught her eating salad on the dining room table. Realizing everything Ophelia had been through, I hadn't resorted to harsh punishment for the offense. Instead, I had made Ophelia a small salad of her own, then gently picked her up and sat her down on the floor beside the bowl.

Ophelia finally wanted to ride in the car again, so I bought her a new harness and leash. At Christmastime, we drove by the med center and on past the towers that had once been her home with Miss Janet.

She still "Mow, Mowed," at four a.m. sometimes as she had with Miss Janet, but I didn't get up with her. Ophelia usually just hopped back into bed to snuggle up behind my knees.

The clincher finally came on the evening I was taking a nap before dinner. I'd just begun dozing off when I felt Ophelia jump up onto the sofa at my feet. Deciding to see what

Ophelia's intentions were, I laid perfectly still, pretending to be asleep. First one paw then another touched my body as I felt Ophelia's breathing coming closer to my face. Ophelia very gently "sniffed me under the nose" in an effort to make sure I was still breathing. In that instant, I knew that Ophelia had finally bonded with me. Tears streamed down my face as I spoke to Ophelia, telling her "how much I loved her and that things would be all right." No one would ever hurt her again. Ophelia really had found a new mom.

THE PROMISE

Faye and Miss Kitty first met when the white long-haired kitten appeared on her neighbor Ann's doorstep as a stray. Miss Kitty as Ann called her, pretty much kept her distance when it came to strangers, Faye included. At the time Miss Kitty appeared on the scene, Faye and Ann had been neighbors for a number of years.

It was soon apparent who Miss Kitty had chosen to be her new mom. Over the years, Miss Kitty and Ann developed the special bond that only comes with much love and understanding.

When Ann became ill with cancer, Miss Kitty was always there. She stayed beside Ann during the times she had to rest from exhaustion brought on by her illness and the accompanying treatments. Miss Kitty remained Ann's constant companion until her death one winter day.

A year prior to her death, Ann had made arrangements with Faye for Miss Kitty's care when she was no longer there for her. Ann had realized that it just wasn't enough to assume that Faye, her children, or anyone else would automatically care for Miss Kitty after she was gone. Faye already had two cats of her own and couldn't take Miss Kitty, but she promised Ann that, "She would see Miss Kitty was well taken care of."

After Ann's death, a grieving Miss Kitty sat endlessly at the back door, waiting to go into the home she'd shared with her late owner. Miss Kitty faithfully stayed on the porch where she warmed herself in the sun and kneaded her paws into the mat in anticipation of Ann's opening the door for her.

Faye began checking on Miss Kitty several times a day. She would brush her, feed her, talk to her and carry her around, in addition to sweeping the porch. She had made a commitment to a friend and was determined to keep it.

Even Faye knew the inevitable would happen someday. Ann's house was finally sold and the new owners would be moving in soon. She became even more determined to find Miss Kitty a good home.

In spite of the fact that numerous people had expressed an interest in adopting the beautiful white cat with tan markings, Faye was reluctant to just give her to anyone. Miss Kitty had grown up around older women, so she knew it would be a major adjustment for her to move into a family setting.

Faye remained determined to fulfill her promise to Ann before her death and began putting up posters with Miss Kitty's face around town. She was not going to let Miss Kitty go to the animal shelter or end up being rejected by a newly adoptive family. Faye even went as far as to tell the interviewees that, "if Miss Kitty didn't work out in a new home, she would take her back." She really stuck to her guns in the search for just the right home for Miss Kitty. She'd made a commitment to a friend and stood by it.

In her search for Miss Kitty's new home, Faye even enlisted the help of a local newspaper reporter to do a feature story in the human interest section of the paper.

Thanks to Faye's love and concern, Miss Kitty finally found a new home with a wonderful family who understood her dilemma.

Sadly, there are scores of cases like Miss Kitty's involving abandoned animals that have tragic endings. The tragedy occurs when a cat or dog is mistakenly put into a situation, such as Ophelia's, where it can be abandoned, abused, neglected or sold for laboratory experimentation.

Companion animals are fraudulently obtained by people answering "Free to Good Home" ads in the newspapers. These people are very persuasive and friendly. They know the right answers to all the questions, because they commit fraud on a regular basis.

A major industry exists in which pets are stolen or obtained under false pretenses then sold to research institutions. Many cats and dogs used in experiments are procured by theft and misrepresentation by middlemen who make a living selling them for research.

Thieves sell stolen animals to dealers and research facilities that are licensed or registered by the U. S. Department of Agriculture's Animal and Plant Health Inspection Service.

Although the AWA discourages pet theft by requiring licensed animal dealers to keep records that help trace lost or stolen pets, it hasn't remedied the situation. Pet owners also have to be responsible in preventing animal theft.

When you aren't at home, keep pets indoors. Provide proper identification with a tag, or in some cases, a tattoo. Microchips are also an option.

Report any suspicious strangers driving around your neighborhood to the police. Alert your neighbors to the problem of pet theft.

Cats should not be allowed to roam freely, while dogs should be outside in fenced yards only for limited periods of time. Take a color photograph of your pet and write down its identifying marks, color, breed and size.

Maintain a list of the phone numbers of local pounds, shelters and other animal assistance facilities. Newspaper offices, radio and television stations sometimes have lost-and-found departments. Dog wardens, police and other officials may also help locate a lost or stolen pet.

Start looking for a missing pet immediately. Put up lost-pet posters and information in your neighborhood. Inquire with local neighbors and have children be on the lookout for your missing pet.

Don't give up on your search. Stray animals can often return to their old neighborhoods weeks after they first disappear.

The best guidelines to use when placing an animal into a new home are similar to those followed by Faye in the case of Miss Kitty. The prospective new owners are interviewed, required to provide secure, accurate information, including an address and phone number.

When adopting from an animal shelter, the applicant is asked numerous questions to make certain they understand the responsibility they are assuming. Written approval from a landlord is often requested. Checking out the prospective new owner's references, visiting the premises and having the new owner sign a pet adoption contract are also recommended.

Adoption fees at shelters can vary from $50.00 to $75.00, depending upon what medical services are provided. The fee usually covers current vaccinations, deworming and spaying/neutering. Middlemen selling animals to labs for profit will be unwilling to pay an adoption fee, even if its a requested donation to a local shelter.

Pets should not be adopted out around Halloween, especially solid black or solid white cats. Most animal shelters give public notice of this policy to the news media, in addition to advising people not to run "Free to Good Home" advertisements.

Tragedy is preventable. Don't carelessly abandon an animal to a random death.

BENNY, BETTY AND RAMBO

Mrs. Roberts was a retired administrator who had been widowed for a number of years. She lived in a high rise condominium which she shared with her three cats, Benny, Betty and Rambo. Benny was a pedigreed persian cat that had originally been purchased as a "lap cat" for Mrs. Roberts aged mother, while Betty and Rambo had been shelter adoptees.

Rambo was a large neutered tomcat with some tabby markings. He made life miserable for his two housemates. Betty, a small, shy gray female was afraid and withdrawn from everyone but Mrs. Roberts. Both she and Benny always made it a point to avoid Rambo whenever possible, since he was the bully of the house. He was indeed the top cat. Rambo would hiss and swipe at both Benny and Betty. He'd also been known to periodically attack Mrs. Roberts with no apparent provocation. Hence, she'd dubbed him "the cat from hell". Despite his shortcomings and tempermental disposition, Mrs. Roberts had refused to give Rambo up, because he'd been a gift from her late husband.

During her career, Mrs. Roberts always ran a "tight ship", so to speak. Everything she'd been responsible for had been strictly by the book, with no loose ends.

Her personal affairs had also been matter-of-fact, except when it came to her Last Will and Testament. Her bequests of specific personal items had been detailed to include everything from her diamond engagement ring to her Seiko watch. All her tangible personal property not disposed of within her detailed bequests had been subsequently listed as clothing, books, personal effects, furniture, furnishings and household possessions. There were also specific instructions governing the division of these remaining assets. Mrs. Robert's will had covered every item except for the three companions who had shared her daily life. Her provision for Benny, Betty and Rambo had only been verbal instructions to her neighbor that all three cats were to be euthanized upon her death.

If an animal is extremely old or in poor health, euthanasia may be the most humane alternative. In such a clear case, forcing an animal to adjust to a new person or circumstances can only compound its suffering, particularly when it has just lost its own human companion.

Advance personal arrangements with a friend or neighbor such as those made by Mrs. Roberts are necessary. These arrangements also need to be confirmed by clear instructions within your will.

Courts are reluctant to destroy pets by order of their deceased owners. There have been cases where a person knew full well that a pet was very old and unadoptable. There would be no one to properly attend to its infirmaties and special needs. Because there were no clear and specific instructions made in advance for someone to euthanize the sick animal immediately upon the owner's death, the case was caught up in court proceedings.

In the case of Benny, Betty and Rambo, Mrs. Roberts wishes were only carried out with regard to Rambo. He was an unadoptable cat who could be harmful to others, hence the neighbor in charge had no alternative but to have a local veterinarian euthanize Rambo the day after Mrs. Roberts passed away. Mrs. Roberts had died suddenly from an aneurysm only two days before Thanksgiving. Faced with her sudden death at such an awkward time, the neighbor had temporarily taken Benny and Betty to her condo with three other cats. In all the confusion, she knew that in spite of what her dear friend had instructed, she couldn't euthanize Beny and Betty.

After many sleepless nights of knowing she couldn't keep Benny and Betty, a thought came to mind. Mrs. Robert's neighbor remembered a conversation they'd had shortly before her death. Mrs. Roberts had been going to the funeral of her secretary's only son. It had been a terrible loss, but the neighbor felt that she should contact the lady. Maybe she would know someone who could help place Benny and Betty?

Betty ended up as an early Christmas gift to the grieving mother and widow who was 84 years old at the time. The shy little gray cat entered her life just a month after her only child had died suddenly. Everyone needs someone to love and care for. Little Betty became the most important part of a grieving woman's life.

Within moments of her arrival at her new home, Betty had darted under the sofa where she stayed hidden, terrified of her surroundings. After two days, Mrs. Robert's secretary had coaxed her out with food. Betty finally began to feel at home. The shy, little gray cat slowly came out from under the sofa to sit beside the one who needed her most. She and Mrs. Robert's secretary developed a very special bond in which Betty helped her through the holidays and her grief. Her love for Betty began filling the empty space that had been left in her life.

In the meantime, Benny was sharing the neighbor's condo with her three cats. When the door was opened, he'd sadly walk up to the door of his old home and cry for his mom to let him in. He didn't understand why he'd suddenly been taken across the hall to a strange place with three other cats.

Christmas drew near and Benny still didn't know that Mrs. Roberts was gone. The neighbor cried for hours after watching him go down the hall to his old home, searching for his mom and his companions. It broke her heart not only for Benny, Betty and Rambo, but because she'd lost a dear friend.

Prevailing upon the kindness of a co-worker, she found a tentative home for Benny shortly after the new year. She'd all but taken him to his new home, when she learned that the prospective adopter had two large dogs who'd never been exposed to cats. Her immediate reaction to placing the meek persian Benny into that situation had been a negative one. Although she was over the limit on the number of cats she was allowed to own, Benny stayed with her.

Fortunately for all concerned, fate stepped in that spring. Mrs. Robert's neighbor lost one of her cats to an illness and Benny was no longer an illegal tenant at the condo. He would remain with his new family forever.

One could say the story had a happy ending, but not over time. Betty had been placed with an 84 year-old owner. Was that wrong? No, because no one can accurately predict whether an owner will outlive a cat or vice-versa. Mrs. Robert's secretary had needed Betty's love and companionship. She thanked the neighbor over and over for giving her Betty.

The neighbor's concern ended up being that she could once again be faced with the possibility of finding a home for Betty, a shy cat who'd been forced to make a difficult adjustment after Mrs. Robert's death. If anything ever happened to her new owner, she'd be back at the condo.

Should Mrs. Robert's wishes to euthanize all three cats have been honored after her death? Why hadn't she included specific instructions regarding Benny, Betty and Rambo with all the detailed requests in her Last Will and Testament?

LAST WILL AND TESTAMENT OF MRS. ROBERTS

"Being of sound mind, I do make, publish and declare this document to be my Last Will and Testament, thereby revoking any codicils, will or other testamentary documents I have made.

I direct my executor to pay out of my residuary estate, all of my just debts, funeral expenses and expenses of administering my estate.

I give and bequeath certain specific items to the below named beneficiaries as follows:

My diamond engagement ring to my beloved neice.
My automobile to my beloved nephew.
My diamond necklace to my beloved sister.
My Seiko watch to my beloved sister.

I also bequeath all of my tangible personal property not mentioned in the preceeding paragraphs which is owned by me at the time of my death, including but not limited to clothing, books, personal effects, furnishings and household possessions, in addition to all insurance policies to my sister, my neice and my nephew in equal shares.

My executor shall distribute my residuary estate or the proceeds therefrom as follows:

One-third to my sister.
One-third to my neice.
One-third to my nephew.

I request the attesting witnesses to my will to subscribe a joint affadavit in accordance with provisions of the law, for the purpose of proving this will when it is offered for probate."

MONEY AND MORALITY

"They life to thy neighbor's creed has lent.
All are needed by each one.
Nothing is fair or good alone."
                    Ralph Waldo Emerson
                    1803-1882

A spirit of goodwill toward others is usually expressed in activities that promote social welfare. Ancient societies often had state-sanctioned measures to aid the poor, infirm and disadvantaged. Many of the world's great religions including Buddhism, Christianity and Islam have always encouraged and recognized the duty of the materially well-off individual to help the less fortunate.

The leading American philanthropist of the Eighteenth Century was Benjamin Rush. Rush was a physician during the Yellow Fever Epidemic of 1793.

In 1866, The American Society for the Prevention of Cruelty to Animals and The Society for Prevention of Cruelty to Children were both founded by American reformer Henry Bergh. Bergh had been a diplomat in the U.S. delegation to Russia under President Lincoln. His passion was to "speak for those who could not speak for themselves." The ASPCA was modeled after England's Royal SPCA and went on to become the oldest humane organization in the Western Hemisphere.

Although she didn't found an organization as far reaching as the ASPCA, local philanthropist Jenny Smith loved animals and other human beings. She'd been gifted with the same passion as Henry Bergh. The President of a corporation she'd owned with her late husband, Jenny donated money to a variety of charities.

She built a house for homeless people to get off the streets. Without her help, there would have been no hot meals, showers, or a warm place to stay for many people who were down on their luck.

Like most animal lovers, Jenny always enjoyed the breakfast hour she spent with her pets. They'd while away the morning hours in her huge dining room unless she had an important meeting to attend. Jenny had been brought up in a home where animals weren't allowed in the dining room or kitchen. Much to the dismay of her assistant and driver, the rules were always broken when it came to the beloved pets who shared her life.

A day never went by that Jenny didn't think of the endless suffering of abandoned animals. Never dreaming that her own pets would some day end up there, she had established a trust fund for the benefit of forgotten animals at the local shelter.

One would assume that since she was the President of a corporation, her Last Will and Testament would have been "ironclad". In some ways it was, but in the most important ways, it was not.

Assuming that she had acquired sufficient knowledge with which to manage her personal affairs, Jenny hand typed her own will. She had included complicated and detailed instructions regarding the disposition of her assets in the event of her death.

Article I directed that all her just debts, funeral expanses and costs in connection with probate be paid. She had also empowered her son as Co-Executor to settle all claims against the estate.

The will went on to address taxes, taxable property and assets receivable. The benefits of tax laws and applicable exemptions were more than adequately discussed.

Jenny had listed her tangible personal property as household furniture, furnishings, automobiles, books, pictures, jewelry, art objects, collections, wearing apparel and other articles of household use or ornament. All articles of personal property listed in the will had been given to her son.

She authorized her Co-Executor to sell all of her capital stock as soon as the sale could be transacted without a loss. The Executors and Co-Executor were given full and complete discretion as to the manner and price for which the stock was sold.

Article VI gave trustees authority to pay or apply for the benefit of her son, part or all the principal of a trust if it became necessary for his health, support and maintenance. Upon the death of her son, the trustees were instructed to divide the trust

72

property into as many separate equal trusts necessary so that a trust would be named for each grandchild she had. The same circumstances and factors regarding distributions of trust income were applicable in the case of the grandchildren.

With respect to Jenny's business holdings, the will contained twenty-nine individually numbered paragraphs filled with minute details regarding the powers granted to the Co-Executor and Trustees.

In accounting, there are two types of errors. The error of commission and the error of omission. An error of comission is done with deliberate intent, while an error of omission is usually an oversight on someone's part. Jenny had not consulted with a legal professional regarding her will and therefore committed two grave oversights. The trust she had established for the local animal shelter had not been incorporated into the terms of her Last Will and Testament. Secondly, there had been no mention whatsoever of her beloved pets in all the detailed paragraphs, sub-paragraphs and clauses intended to convey her wishes.

There are scores of cases that have had tragic endings simply because the person involved did not attend to very critical matters during their lifetime. Because there were no clear and specific instructions or arrangements made in advance, the bank trust department, trustees, lawyers and courts had no jurisdiction in those left out of Jenny's will.

The animal shelter lost valuable funding that they had used to better care for and keep abandoned animals alive longer, some of whom they'd succeeded in placing as a result of Jenny's help. With the funds from the trust no longer available, many animals who might have otherwise found homes were euthanized when their time was up.

The heartbreaking part of the story came on the day an employee of Jenny's company arrived at the shelter with her pets. They had been abandoned by her son, who no longer wanted the obligation of caring for them.

"Money and Morals in America" by Patricia O'Toole recounts the history of the conflict between greed and good in today's society. Ms. O'Toole looks at the dilemma people have faced between the making of money and giving it away to worthy causes. In Jenny's case, there would have been plenty left over for her heirs had they chosen to do the "morally right" thing in honoring her wishes.

LAST WILL AND TESTAMENT OF JENNY SMITH

ARTICLE I

"I, Jenny Smith, do make, publish and declare this to be my Last Will and Testament. I hereby revoke all other wills and codicils I have made.

I direct that all my just debts, funeral expenses and costs connected with probating and distributing my estate be paid as soon as possible after my death. My son is empowered as Co-Executor to settle all claims against my estate.

ARTICLE II

Inheritance, estate and other taxes are to be paid by my Co-Executors to taxing authorities. This shall be apportioned among the persons in accordance with respective values, giving them the benefit of exemptions and deductions allowed by law. Any assets receivable are to be considered in the distribution of the estate.

ARTICLE III

I give to my son, the house in which I currently reside. If he does not survive me, the property shall be added to and distributed in my residuary estate.

ARTICLE IV

I give all tangible property owned by me at the time of my death including household furnishings, automobiles, books, pictures, jewelry, art objects, collections, wearing apparel and other articles of household use to my son. If he does not survive me, the property shall be added to and distributed in my residuary estate. All costs of packing, storing and safeguarding my personal property before distribution shall be expensed to the administration of my estate.

ARTICLE V

I authorized and empower my Co-Executor to sell the capital stock of my corporation owned by me at my death, as soon as the sale can be transacted without a loss. My Co-Executor is authorized to execute any instrument(s) required to transfer the capital stock.

ARTICLE VI

Subject to the provisions of paragraph 3.7 of Article VI, if my son does not survive me, I bequeath my residuary estate to my Co-Trustee to be held and administered in accordance with the provisions of the trust held for my grandchildren.

ARTICLE VII

My Co-Trustees shall administer the proceeds from capital stock sales as I have previously directed. The Co-Trustees may apply part or all of the principal for the benefit of my son during his lifetime. On the death of my son, the Trustee will divide the trust property into as many separate equal trusts necessary for my grandchildren at the time. The trustee may also distribute principal amounts for the needs of each child specified. Each trust established receives S-Corporation stock that shall be distributed to the income beneficiary of that trust.

ARTICLE VIII

Paragraphs 1-29, "minute" details regarding the powers granted to Co-Executors and Trustees. My son shall have the exclusive right to vote all the capital stock held by my estate. I nominate him and the bank as my Co-Executors.
*Animal Shelter Trust Not Incorporated Into Terms of Will

I hereby request that the attesting witnesses to this document make and subscribe a joint affidavit in accordance with applicable laws. In Witness Whereof, I sign and seal this document, together with the attestations, it was typewritten by me upon 44 pages of paper, one face thereof. I have signed my name at the bottom of each page for authentication and identification."

Jenny Smith (Seal)

THE KENNEDY ORPHANS

The nation was stunned when John F. Kennedy Jr., his wife Caroyn Bessette Kennedy and sister-in-law Lauren were suddenly killed in a plane crash. The Kennedy's dog Friday and cat Ruby were unaware they had lost their masters.

Friday, whom the couple had said they rescued from a shelter, was in reality, a purebred Canaan. In an attempt to protect Friday's breed from people seeking to make a profit, JFK Jr. had portrayed him as a pound puppy. Friday often protected Carolyn when the paparazzi followed her around New York.

Ruby had belonged to Carolyn before she married JFK Jr.. Along with Friday, Ruby had become a beloved family pet who lived with John and Carolyn in their Tribeca neighborhood apartment in New York City.

When JFK Jr.'s will was filed in Manhattan Surrogate's Court on September 24, 1999, it contained a detailed list of family, friends and charities who would receive money from his estate.

At the time of his death, JFK Jr. had wanted most of his worldly possessions to go to his wife and children. His wife was also killed in the plane crash and there were no children.

His sister, Carolina Kennedy Schlossberg and her three children were therefore the prime beneficiaries of his will. The Tribeca apartment and "personal belongings" went to Caroline's children. His nephew received a piece of property identified in the will and a carved scrimshaw collection that had once belonged to President John F. Kennedy.

Cousins Timothy Shriver and Robert F. Kennedy Jr. were also named in the will. Shriver became executor of JFK Jr.'s estate.

Kennedy had included bequests to his childhood nanny, a family butler, and his personal assistant at "George Magazine". His late father's presidential library and the charity Reaching Up Inc., which he founded to help mentally disabled people were also remembered.

Although the exact value of the estate remained unclear, the bulk of the assets were directed to a trust that had been established in 1983. Most of the beneficiaries were paid from the fund, known as the John F. Kennedy Jr. 1983 Trust.

John F. Kennedy Jr.'s will was only 3 1/2 pages long and bequeathed assets estimated to be about $50,000,000.00 to his beneficiaries. However, no mention was ever made of the family pets, Friday and Ruby.

Like many orphaned companion animals, Friday and Ruby didn't understand why their masters never returned. They were more fortunate than others, in that they did find new homes with people who loved them.

A PRAYER FOR MOMMA

"He giveth to the beast his food
and to the young ravens which cry."

Psalms 147:9

The Great Kanawha River received its name from an indian tribe which once dwelt in West Virginia. Throughout the years, the river served as a hub for barge transportation with connections from the Ohio and Mississippi rivers to The Gulf of Mexico. In modern times, it beckons to boaters and swimmers of all ages.

Although the river looks inviting, it often has debris and an undertow that can overcome even the strongest swimmer. Such was the case one Saturday afternoon in June when an inexperienced swimmer became trapped and dropped out of sight after calling for help several times.

Bystanders had already dialed 911 when Charlie jumped into the water to rescue the drowning man. When police and firefighters arrived on the scene, both men had been pulled under by the river's current.

After a brief search, they recovered both victims and pulled them up onto the river's edge. Resuscitation was attempted immediately and Charlie was quickly transported to a local hospital. He was pronounced dead 30 minutes after arrival.

Drowning is death by suffocation caused by water in the respiratory system. Resuscitation by artificial respiration can prevent death if begun quickly. Because of the constant need of body tissue for oxygen, even a few minutes of suffocation can result in brain damage or death to a victim.

A follow-up investigation by police found that Charlie had jumped into the river to save the swimmer who had cried out for help. The panic stricken victim had then fought his rescuer, ultimately resulting in a watery death for both.

Charlie's survivors had included his ex-wife, two adult children who lived out-of-state and a sister. He had been homeless for a brief period following his divorce and finally managed to rent a small apartment with the money he earned as a short order cook at a local fast food restaurant.

At the time of his death, the only living being who shared Charlie's life was a bedraggled looking mutt he'd named "Momma" because of her obvious condition. Charlie had first met "Momma" out behind the restaurant foraging for food one night. She'd later accompanied him home. From that day forward, "Momma" had feasted on leftover burgers, fries, chicken and other delicacies.

Unbeknownst to anyone involved, Momma dog had given birth to eight puppies the night after Charlie had died. Since he had died "intestate", or without a will, "Momma" and her puppies weren't discovered for several days.

Charlie's sister had been quite surprised when she entered the tiny apartment and was greeted by the cries of eight new lives coming from a closet. Sadly, she knew what their fate would be. Charlie's children wouldn't want "Momma" and her babies, nor would his ex-wife. There was no money with which to care for them and only a few personal items of no value left in the apartment "Momma" had shared with Charlie.

"Momma" and her puppies were transported to the local shelter where they were well cared for. Four of the eight puppies found new homes, while "Momma" and the others were euthanized when their time was up.

When a person dies without a will, or if a person's will is determined by the courts to be invalid, any property is distributed in accordance with individual state laws. Intestate succession, as it is called, results in the state probate court appointing someone to administer the deceased person's estate. The appointed administrator has to obtain a surety bond in order to insure the estate against misappropriation by the administrator. The estate pays any premium charged for the bond.

An administrator is required to collect all estate assets and pay legitimate debts, claims and expenses of administering the estate. All death taxes are included. The court appointed administrator is also entitled to a commission for services rendered. After the debts of the estate are paid, the administrator then distributes any remaining assets to the deceased person's "heirs at law".

An individual state's intestancy laws determine a deceased person's heirs, or next of kin. Spouses usually receive one-half of the estate, while children and other descendants are entitled to the remainder. If there is no surviving spouse, children usually receive the entire estate. Parents are next in line, followed by more distant relatives. If there are no relatives, an individual's estate reverts back to the particular state where he/she resided at the time of death. In very rare cases, property can pass by intestancy to the same person(s) designated as beneficiaries in a will.

In Charlie's case, there had been no assets besides clothing he wore to work and his best friend Momma who had brightened up the last few months of his life.

ANGEL OF THE BADLANDS

"The Badlands" was a small community consisting of numerous bars, businesses and strip clubs scattered along U.S. Route 60 between Spring Hill and St. Albans, W.Va.. The area was so named, because it was known as a haven for drug dealing and other criminal activity.

I drove through The Badlands on my way to work every day, because it was five miles shorter than taking the interstate. Traveling through The Badlands enabled me to avoid the stress of fighting bumper-to-bumper traffic. Given the intense summer heat during 1988, driving the shorter distance without having to sit in a car for hours had been a blessing.

The long, hot summer of that year played host to the worst drought in fifty years. People were ordered to take water conservation measures, so they stopped washing cars and watering lawns. The intense heat finally shattered several of the huge concrete slabs that made up the four-lane highway through The Badlands.

Located a short distance from the broken pavement was an auto graveyard. Complete with its broken-down rusty fence and abandoned hulks of old wrecked cars, the junkyard had long been an eyesore in the community.

A shabby looking old house trailer with several mangy dogs tied outside sat nearby. The front yard was strewn with trash and junk. Why someone would choose to live there would be a mystery to outsiders, but in The Badlands, people were known to take what they could get.

Five adults were crammed together inside the giant tin can. With only a small fan circulating the hot air, the rickety trailer had been a virtual "sweat box". Cockroaches scurried around the kitchen, while rats raced past the barking dogs outside, occasionally stopping to rummage through the trash.

The only other occupant of the trailer had been a kitten named "Sunshine". The pretty little blotched tabby was a birthday gift to Cindy that summer. She had called her Sunshine, because she'd given her the only happiness in her life.

Cindy had been divorced that spring and spent the long, hot summer in the trailer with her mother, brothers and a local Badlands resident named "Mean Man" because she had nowhere else to go.

During her brief stint at the trailer, Cindy had dated two men who after brief courtships, had simply disappeared from her life. Sunshine had been the only one she could rely on. Unbeknownst to Cindy, a series of sinister events had begun taking place on the hot summer nights she spent with Sunshine.

Under cover of darkness, Mean Man frequently ventured across the highway to hang out in an old abandoned motel across from the auto graveyard. Once the site of many liaisons and rendezvous, it had long since closed its doors. Due to the dilapidated condition of the building, sheets of plywood had been nailed over the windows to keep out intruders. That of course, meant any intruders except for Mean Man. He'd forced open the back door with the stalk of his shotgun and used the motel's interior walls for target practice more than once.

Shots rang out all hours of the night, which wasn't uncommon in The Badlands. People rarely phoned police, fearing that if it were a real crime, they wouldn't want to be involved.

Because no one notified law enforcement of Mean Man's activities, he began a series of systematic, bloody, violent assassinations that were carried out from the blazing summer months until January of the following year. Occupants of the trailer mysteriously disappeared, along with Cindy's two ex boyfriends and eventually, Cindy herself.

No one paid any attention to Mean Man or his comings and goings. It was, after all, no one's business.

The catalyst which first brought authorities to the run down trailer had been the emaciated condition of the dogs tied up outside. Shortly before Thanksgiving, animal cruelty charges were brought against several of the trailer's occupants. During a raid by Sheriff's deputies and animal control officers, the starving dogs were seized and taken to the animal shelter.

No one knew about Sunshine until animal control officers searched the inside of the premises and found her barely alive.

Sunshine hadn't been fed or watered since the night Cindy disappeared.

Hearings were scheduled on the cruelty charges, but none of the defendants would show up. This subsequently prompted an investigation into the whereabouts of the starved animals' owners.

In the meantime, all of the dogs seized in the raid were euthanized. As a result of living in such deplorable conditions, they had suffered from acute dehydration and malnutrition as well as skin infections.

The lone survivor from the raid on the trailer had been a "very pregnant" Sunshine. Although she wasn't euthanized, Sunshine remained near death. Further complicating matters, the lives of her kittens were also at stake.

Maternal malnutrition is magnified in animals when compared to human beings. The magnitude of dietary deprivation in animal experimentation is rarely if ever seen in human beings.

Sunshine's caretakers at the animal shelter had been prepared for her organs to shut down. They realized it wouldn't be anything they could help, but at the same time, everyone involved in her recovery had been pulling for her.

There were many setbacks during Sunshine's recovery period, including when she lost her kittens. Considering what she'd been through, the loss of her kittens had been no surprise to her caretakers.

By the time she began eating on her own, Sunshine's growth had been stunted from the malnutrition she'd suffered. In addition to loosing her kittens, she'd almost died from heart, kidney and liver failure. She still needed lots of love and care, which lead the animal shelter director to make an important decision regarding her welfare. She would not be placed up for adoption, but would instead remain at the shelter forever.

Since no one knew that her dead owner had called her Sunshine, her new name became "Rutty Lou". "Rutty" for short, found a wonderful new home with the folks at the shelter.

In the meantime, yellow crime scene tape surrounded the old abandoned motel down in The Badlands. The dark gray winter sky made things look even more dismal to passing motorists. Assisted by a local psychic, several bodies were found by police, among them was Sunshine's owner, Cindy. Another body was eventually located in the auto graveyard across the highway.

Mean Man was subsequently sentenced to life in prison without parole for two of six murders. Although he'd been charged in connection with Cindy's death, he professed not to know anything about it.

Rutty Lou, a.k.a. Sunshine, still resides at the local animal shelter, oblivious to the fact that her mom was a murder victim. When you walk in the front door, you are greeted by a charming, small, blotched tabby who has more finesse than the professional greeters at Wal Mart.

UNLOVED, UNWANTED AND UNWELCOME

Feral cats are more often than not, the offspring of domestic cats that have been abandoned by humans. Contrary to what some people assume, a domestic cat does not automatically revert to its wild instincts and cannot fend for itself without a home.

These cats frequently die violent, painful deaths as strays from starvation, disease, abuse and as food for predators. A pair of breeding cats can have two or more litters of kittens a year. Over a seven-year period, this exponentially produces a total of 420,000 offspring.

People from humane and veterinary organizations attempt to help feral cats by feeding, trapping, neutering and inoculating them. The tame cats are placed in shelters for adoption, while those too wild to interact with human beings are returned to the feral cat areas.

In the real world, feral cats are ignored, neglected and pushed aside. Because they do not have homes, they become unloved, unwanted and unwelcome by humans.

Humorist H. Allen Smith wrote a 1946 novel about a cat named "Rhubarb". Rhubarb was a rangy, muscular feral cat, said to be the color of yellow smoke. He first revealed himself alongside a hedge which bordered a six-hole golf course. At the time, he was stalking a dog which was being led by its mistress, a Miss Rebecca Ross.

Rhubarb continued his advances toward the dog, despite Miss Ross yelling, "Scat!" Typical of feral cat behavior, a fearless Rhubarb leapt onto the dog with his forelegs spread wide, all the while emitting a spinechilling screach.

Miss Ross later described Rhubarb as an "ordinary alley cat, bigger than most, with a large head and a crooked tail." His long yellow tail was said to have looked like a door might have been slammed on it.

The headlines of the morning newspaper read:

The police were on the lookout for a large yellow cat that had been assaulting neighborhood dogs. Women in the area reported that the yellow cat hid behind bushes and trees where he could spring upon unsuspecting dogs. His assaults had been described as "ferocious".

In defense of Rhubarb's behavior, a Mrs. Marilynn Hackle, whose title Mr. Smith gave as, "the Exalted Pussy of the Queens County Cat Lover's League", issued a statement condemming police action in Rhubarb's case. Mrs. Hackle had said that, "the cat was not to be blamed for his conduct. He had been mistreated by someone. He had not been given the love and affection that was the inalienable right of all cats. Consequently, Rhubarb was nervous and upset. Modern society was considerate of human beings who became emotionally unstable and recognized that they were sick. Why not cats?"

After reading the article, eccentric millionaire Thaddeus Whitcomb Banner decided he wanted Rhubarb for his household pet. He had admired Rhubarb's guts and courage. With orders to "find the cat, no matter what it takes!" Thaddeus Banner's assistant Eric hit the streets in search of Rhubarb.

Eric pondered how he was going to apprehend such a cat. He first ordered a special collapsible net, then borrowed a friend's dog, which he walked in the park to entice Rhubarb. He hung out at the tennis club, where a man told him that the cat, "stole tennis balls from people." He ran into a young boy who told him, "people were scared to death."

When Eric inquired if Rhubarb ever attacked people, he was told, "only mailmen." Eric told people he was a G-man to get information about Rhubarb.

Eric finally found Rhubarb's hideout near the clubhouse. It was a small cavelike hole, camouflaged with leaves, sticks and weeds. Inside were approximately 30 tennis balls and 15 golf balls. Rhubarb was nowhere in sight, so Eric put up his net and waited for the cat to return. He was there all night and part of the next day, but he didn't catch Rhubarb.

He left and returned the next day with a trap, which he placed near the edge of the clubhouse grounds instead of close to Rhubarb's cave. He baited the trap with six new tennis balls and six new golf balls.

Rhubarb was in the trap by the next morning. No one ever knew what happened to the fierce yellow cat and members of the tennis club talked about Rhubarb's attacks for two years afterward. Some speculated that he had crept into his cave and choked to death on one of the tennis balls he'd stolen.

Thaddeus Banner had welcomed Rhubarb into his home with wide-eyed delight. Once the wooden cat trap had been set down, the cat had slashed the wooden slats with needle-sharp claws, tore out chunks with his teeth and snarled like a lion. Thaddeus laughed so hard tears ran down his cheeks.

Rhubarb got his name from a colloquialism insinuated into Yankee vernacular by baseball broadcaster Red Barber. A "rhubarb" was a noisy altercation, a brawl, a violent emotional upheaval brought on by epical dispute.

Thaddeus Banner tamed Rhubarb by violating all the rules. He shouted the cat into temporary submission, then slapped him knock-kneed until Rhubarb recognized his master and came to love him.

Beyond Thaddeus and Eric, Rhubarb had no tolerance for any other living creature. Whenever he was taken out in public by Eric or Thaddeus, he was on a thin, short leash made of strongest silk.

Thaddeus Whitcomb Banner died forty-eight hours after he'd signed his last will and testament. His heart stopped as he sat in his big leather chair with his beloved Rhubarb on his lap.

Eric was lying in bed smoking a cigarette when the call came. Thaddeus Banner's daughter Myra was standing in front of a cabinet with an upraised broom drawn on Rhubarb when he arrived at the Banner residence. "Pop's gone now and I'll kill that damed cat if its the last thing I do. This is my house now." It suddenly dawned on Eric that Myra hadn't been informed of her father's last will and testament.

He had to inform Myra "that her father had practically disinherited her. Rhubarb got almost everything. She would only be receiving an income of five-thousand dollars a year from the estate, nothing more."

When the lawyer arrived, he advised Myra Banner that, "her father had dictated the contents of the will and that he would merely read the words and the testator."

LAST WILL AND TESTAMENT OF THADDEUS WHITCOMB BANNER

"I hesitate to think what the said Myra Banner would do with my money and properties. I confess freely that, for some reason beyond my grasp, I have no more affection for her than she has for me. I believe there is bad blood in her. I have always wanted to establish a proper relationship, as is normal between father and daughter, but it has been impossible. I have had to turn elsewhere for that companionship and affection that she withheld from me. I have had to turn to Rhubarb Banner. He has given me love unsparingly. He has been a solace to me in my old age. He is not, it is true, a human being, but I believe him to be in many respects better and more noble than a human being. He is incapable of holding a dagger in his paws, but, assuming he could learn to hold one, and I doubt not that he could learn it, he would not use it to stab me in the back I have not affection whatever for any member of the human race and I die in bitterness, a bitterness that is tempered only by the admiration and respect I hold for the said Rhubarb Banner. He has served me well in life, and I intend that he shall serve me well when I am gone. To him I bequeath the residue of my property, including Banner Athletic Enterprises. I realize full well that he is not altogether capable of administering the estate I am leaving to him. If he had the power of speech, so that human beings could understand his will, I would not hesitate. It is necessary, therefore, that I appoint a guardian for the said Rhubarb Banner. For this task I designate my friend and employee, Eric Yeager. In my estimation the said Eric Yeager comes nearest to being a passable human being of anyone I know. Moreover, he is the only human being who commands the respect and affection of said Rhubarb Banner. He is, so far as I know, worthy of my trust. Therefore, he is to be guardian of the said Rhubarb Banner. He is to support and maintain the said Rhubarb Banner in the manner and style to which the said Rhubarb Banner is accustomed. Acting as guardian, the said

Eric Yeager is to have full charge of all business matters and is to act for and in the interest of the said Rhubarb Banner.

In the full possession of my faculties, I demand that the terms of this last will and testament be carried out to the letter. I want no cheap flabbymouthed lawyers tampering with my decisions as expressed herein. I want none of the low thieves who disgrace the judiciary to upset or try to upset the the terms of my will. I believe I have made my desires clear. If my will is thwarted I hope that from the grave I'll be able to haunt and horrify those responsible for it."

In the story of "Rhubarb", Eric was appointed to be a cat's guardian, because he was the only other human being besides Thaddeus Whitcomb Banner that had commanded Rhubarb's respect over the years. According to the terms of Thadd Banner's last will and testament, Eric was to support and maintain Rhubarb in the manner to which he'd become accustomed.

Rhubarb had inherited millions of dollars and a baseball team. Thus, he'd become a wealthy American Hero, or had he?

THE GUARDIAN

Once the terms of Thaddeus Whitcomb Banner's last will and testament were revealed, Eric had called a press conference in his office. He then recited the bare facts of Thadd's bequest to Rhubarb, which resulted in an instant media frenzy.

One newspaper account had stated that, "No animal was capable of administering the affairs which belong to a man. Let us hope that the courts act wisely in this matter and restore the dignity of man."

Another publication had compared Thaddeus Banner to the Roman Emperor, Caligula who appointed his horse "Incitatus" consul of the Roman Empire. The article had gone on to say that, "Caligula was a mad, perverted, debauched and altogether evil man. It is difficult to believe that in this modern day and age, we should find another human being so contemptuous of mankind as to leave his personal empire to an animal. A cat's normal mission in life is to rid the world of mice, to luxuriate before an open fire, to climb trees, to propagate fluffy kittens and to pose for photographs."

Other "heavy thinkers" of the New York press were not so severe with Thad Banner's wishes. "One ponders the possible effect Mr. Banner's experiment might have on the moneyed class of this nation." He foresaw an "epidemic" of bequests to animals and decried it as "a step toward the collapse of civilization."

The dictionary defines a guardian as, "one that guards, or a custodian. One who has the care of the person or property of another."

The concept of guardianship has been around for over 2,000 years. It is used as a means to ensure that for an individual who cannot give informed consent to determine their own best interests, the next best person is recognized as having legal authority to do so.

A relationship is established between the guardian and the person whose property is being preserved and controlled. Someone's property is managed and controlled by another person under a court order. A guardian is then held responsible for all contracts and can be held personally liable for damages and breach of contract in carrying out his/her duties. A protected person's assets may include homes, cars, life insurance or stocks. The assets are used for the benefit of the protected individual.

The "fatal flaw" in Thaddeus Banner's last will and testament lay in his leaving the bulk of his estate, including a baseball team, directly to Rhubarb. Since Rhubarb was a cat, he was not considered a protected person, but a piece of personal property included in Thadd Banner's estate.

Thadd had appointed Eric as guardian to a piece of personal property in the form of Rhubarb. Eric was to support and maintain Rhubarb with money he did not legally inherit. In the real world, Rhubarb did not inherit any property for Eric to preserve and control, so a guardian relationship failed to exist.

Mr. Banner's reasoning in appointing Eric as Rhubarb's guardian had been that "because Rhubarb didn't have the power of speech, human beings couldn't understand his will." This would have been the case with all companion animals.

Had Rhubarb been a minor child, a guardianship could have easily been created. A parent would have no longer been available to look after his welfare.

Unlike a child, you can leave your cat to someone, but since the cat is considered personal property, it could be treated as if it were a piece of jewelry or an article of clothing. The person could accept it, then sell, destroy or just ignore the cat.

Thadd Banner had felt that Rhubarb was more noble than any human being. He had given him love and been a solace to him in his old age. In the end, Rhubarb was still a cat.

Without someone to look after a pet's welfare, no amount of money will assure proper care after an owner's death. Alternative care must be in place for a pet immediately, or as soon as the owner dies, or is no longer able to properly care for an animal. Most pet owners usually know their own pet's individual needs and can best judge with whom and in what circumstances their pet would be most happy. Hence, Thadd Banner had attempted to appoint Eric to be Rhubarb's guardian after his death. He had just gone about it in the wrong way.

If there are no specific and clear instructions or arrangements made in advance for someone to care for a pet immediately, a case can get bogged down in court proceedings wherein executors end up asking judges to give them instructions. This can result in a long period of anguish for the pet and end up being just the opposite of what the decedent had intended.

In spite of all these considerations, people all too frequently place reliance upon "legalistic solutions" to take care of their pets after they die. Thadd Banner had specified that "Eric Yaeger was to have full charge of all business matters and was to act for and in the interest of Rhubarb." His instructions were meaningless in Rhubarb's case.

The last paragraph of Thadd Banner's will had gone on to demand that the terms of his will be carried out. "In the full possession of my faculties, I demand that the terms of this last will and testament be carried out to the letter. I want no ' "'-P. I want no cheap flabbymouthed lawyers tampering with my decisions as expressed herein. I want none of the low thieves who disgrace the judiciary to upset or try to upset the terms of my will. I believe I have made my desires clear."

To Rhubarb's detriment, Thadd Banner hadn't consulted with his attorney regarding the legality of the terms of his will. He had only "dictated" his wishes and assumed they'd be carried out after his death.

A pet owner should not resort to sophisticated legalistic devices without consulting a local attorney who can advise them on whether their state's laws will recognize and enforce such devices when an animal is the beneficiary. Unless the courts of a particular state have clearly recognized and enforced such trusts or other similar strategems in favor of animals, it is best to seek another legal solution. In any event, even if a trust or some similar legal vehicle is to be used, a pet owner should try to use a caring and knowledgeable person either as trustee or to oversee the trustee in all matters concerning the care of beloved companion animals.

These types of arrangements can still be challanged even if they seem to accomplish what the pet owner wants. If challanged, they are generally not allowed.

People also attempt to make conditional gifts in their wills to take care of their pet, or by setting up a trust with the pet as the beneficiary. These kinds of solutions tend to be of limited use for a number of reasons, including the fact that only a minority of states recognize or enforce trusts having animals as beneficiaries, outright gifts to animals and conditional gifts to another human being for the benefit of an animal. Attempting to use such legalistic solutions, particularly when large sums of money or property are diverted to the care of an animal, invites the legal attack by relatives through a challenge to the will in court. "Myra vs Rhubarb" would prove to be no exception.

"MYRA VS RHUBARB"

A formal challenge in court to the validity of a will is referred to as a contest. This challenge can be based upon a claim that the will was not validly executed. If a will is not properly signed by the testator or not properly witnessed, it can be declared invalid. A will contest can also be based upon the grounds that the testator lacked the legal capacity to execute a will. The challenger would have to prove that the testator was not competent to make a will, was unduly influenced by someone, or a portion of the will was ambiguous and not capable of interpretation.

If a will is carefully drawn up and prepared, it is less likely to be challenged, but there are still no guarantees. Factors that help make a challenge less likely include preparation a good length of time prior to one's death, having the will drawn up while one is still healthy in mind & body. Leaving your estate in accordance with that determined by nature, such as a bequest to relatives with a generous intent also helps prevent hurt feelings in most cases.

Relatives and/or heirs are more likely to challenge wills prepared in the final stage of an illness or which contain unusual dispositions regarding an estate. Leaving everything to a caretaker would be a prime example. Leaving money directly to an animal would be another. The courts could convert the bequest to a trust, or invalidate the entire will.

Shortly after learning the terms of her father's will, a dejected Myra Banner had shrieked, "I'll kill that s.o.b. for certain now!" She had, of course, been referring to Rhubarb.

By the time Myra's challenge to her father's will had made it to the courtroom, it would have seemed impossible that anyone in New York hadn't learned of Rhubarb's plight from the press coverage. However, such a person did in fact, exist. It was Phidias Loudermilk, judge of the Surrogate's Court.

Judge Loudermilk had been secretly engaged in an altruistic project that was to be his contribution to mankind. He had been spending all his spare time in the seclusion of his home, translating words and phrases into Greek.

The judge was sitting on the bench thinking in Greek when the sheriff walked into his chambers with a silver cage in his hands and a big yellow cat inside the cage.

"Well sheriff, what have we here?" said the judge.

"A cat, your honor."

"Did I order a cat?"

"In a way you did, your honor."

"Strange. I have no recollection of it. Let me think." Could it be mice? No really. Sheriff, I feel there must be some mistake."

"Your Honor," said the sheriff with a hint of exasperation, "This here cat is Rhubarb."

"Indeed! He doesn't look it. Are you trying to confuse me?"

"Rhubarb!" The sheriff repeated.

"Rhubarb Banner. Myra Vs Rhubarb. Legatee in same."

The judge pondered the elucidation for a moment. Then he looked closely at the sheriff.

"Judge" said the sheriff, "this is the cat Rhubarb.

The cat that inherited Thadd Banner's estate. The cat that got the ball team. You know judge."

"Bless my soul!" said the judge.

"Does the cat know it?"

"That I couldn't say, your honor. He don't act like he was better than anybody else."

"Fetch him over here. Let's have a look at him."

"Why was it you brought him to me sheriff?"

"You ordered it, your honor. Remember that thing you signed this morning?"

"But I didn't realize-but-well you mean to say this cat is the party I ordered in for examination?"

"Sure, Judge, I thought you knew."

"What is the cat's name again?"

"Rhubarb, your honor, Rhubarb Banner. He's famous Judge. And he's rich. He's I suppose a millionaire."

The Judge searched around in the litter on his desk and came up with some papers labeled, Myra vs Rhubarb. Among them was a copy of Thadd Banner's will. The Judge read the document carefully, then looked at Rhubarb in his cage. "A rather interesting case for a change," he concluded. "I wonder what I should do about it?"

Myra had objected to her father's will and advanced a rather peculiar contention. She avered that rhubarb was not normal. Her contention was that not only had Rhubarb exercised undue influence over her father when he himself was of unsound mind. Myra also alleged that Rhubarb was psychopathic. She cited ancient Chinese and Siamese laws predicated on the belief that the souls of certain humans are transmitted into the bodies of cats after death. She argued that such a reincarnation may have occurred in Rhubarb Banner's case and that he showed every evidence of being possessed by the soul of a madman.

While Eric laughed at Myra's allegations, the Judge had cautioned him. "This is a case without precedent, at least it has no precedent in my experience. It fascinates me and I do not intend to overlook a single contingency."

"It is sufficiently strange in itself that a cat has come into possession of great wealth. Suppose that cat, on top of everything else, is insane? We'll have him examined by a lunacy commission."

During Rhubarb's examination, the two psychiatrists in charge got into their own cat fight. Eric shoved Rhubarb into his cage and they left. They never found out who won the fight.

On the opening day of Myra vs Rhubarb, there was no space left in the courtroom for casual spectators attending the trial. Myra sat at a long shiny table with her husband. At a similar table opposite them sat an attorney with Eric and company. On that table stood the silver cage containing Rhubarb.

The first witness to testify for the defense was a Miss Wood, who was "an expert on cats." Myra's attorney proceeded to ask Miss Wood "How much money Eric Yaeger had paid her for her expert opinions about Rhubarb?"

"Not a cent!" Miss Wood had replied.

"Mr. Lawyer, I am unofficially the mother of all cats in the world. I regard cats for what they are-people."

"Cats are people?"

"Pure and simple," Miss Wood responded.

"A cat is as much a person as you are."

"Cats are people, and the sooner the world accepts that fact, the better off the world will be."

Orlando Dill, one of the baseball players took the stand in Rhubarb's behalf. He testified that "Rhubarb was a fine employer. He'd rather be working for the cat than a human being."

Unlike the sad fates of many companion animals, Rhubarb's story had a happy ending. Judge Loudermilk accepted a psychiatrist's opinion that Rhubarb was indeed sane. After a lot of courtroom examination, it was finally determined that Thaddeus Whitcomb Banner wasn't Myra's natural father. Thadd Banner's wishes were carried out and his beloved Rhubarb got to keep the millions bequeathed to him, along with the baseball team.

The New York Loons became World Champions and Rhubarb rode up lower Broadway in a ticker tape parade. In real life, a judge would have more than likely invalidated Thaddeus Banner's entire last will and testament.

One such case in point went all the way to the California Supreme Court. Roxy Russell was a dog who's owner had left her a bequest of half of her estate. In C. 2d 200, the court ruled the Roxy could not be a beneficiary of the outright gift her owner had made in her will. The court held that the dog Roxy was not eligible to receive an outright gift, even though the legal definition of a "person" included individuals, corporations and charities. The Supreme Court further directed distribution of Roxy's half of the assets to her owner's legal heirs.

The State of New York has since passed legislation which allows individuals to leave property in an honorary trust for a pet. To date, only seven states specifically provide for trusts for animals.

SIAMESE-A-PHOBIA

Simon was a wonderful cat who kept his mom company until the very end. After her death, he spent several weeks with his former owner's grandson before ending up at the local animal shelter. He became yet another victim of someone who didn't want the responsibility of caring for a companion animal.

Mrs. Rose's grandson was a young working man in his late twenties who didn't feel like responding to Simon's cries when he came running with a toy in his mouth. He had left Simon to "fend for himself" in an apartment all day, then expected him to be quiet when he returned home in the evening.

True to his breed, the handsome blue-eyed siamese male was only aloof and demure in appearance. He craved attention and was always "very verbal" in letting his mom know it. His constant siamese "talking" was quite annoying to his new owner, not to mention the lap sitting, sleeping in bed and game playing he'd been accustomed to with his mom. Simon always had constant love and attention from an elderly woman who doted on him. He'd been his mom's best friend for seven years when he lost her.

The fact that Simon was a well mannered, mature cat with an affectionate disposition was of little consequence once he ended up in the shelter. Kittens and puppies are always adopted before older animals.

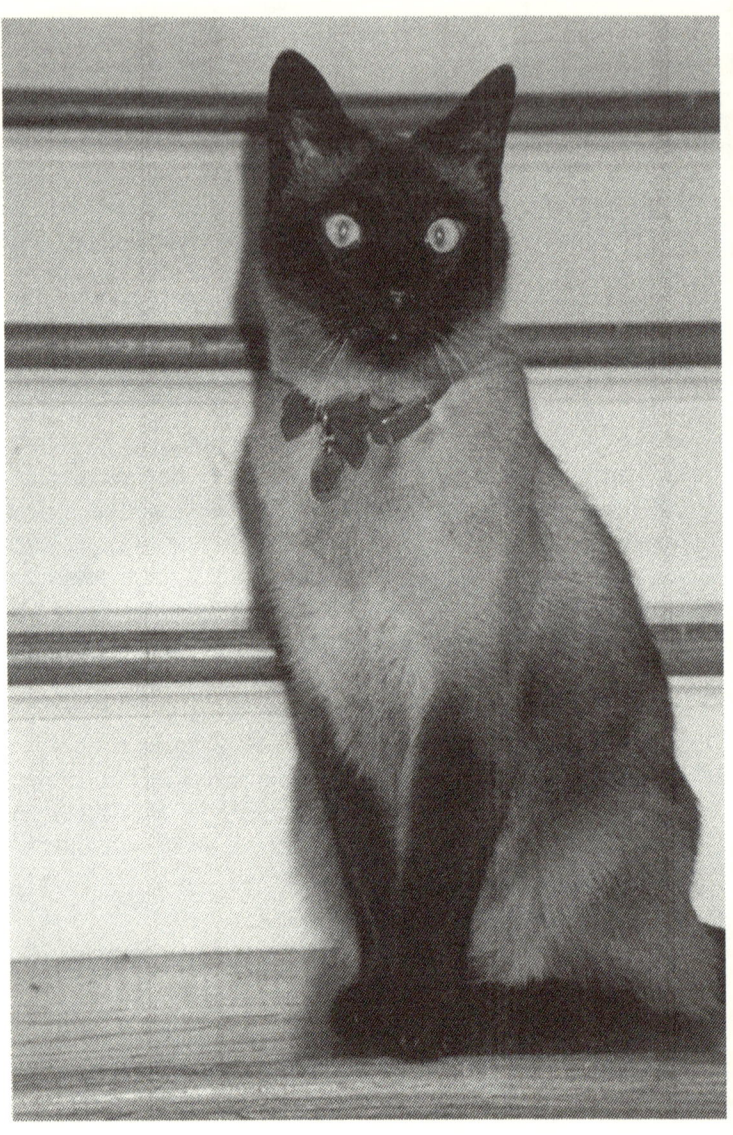

Several visitors to the shelter took Simon out of his cage and into the bonding area to play. Even though it was obvious that he had a very loving disposition, no one ever took him home. This only added to Simon's pain and confusion. His mom was gone, he didn't know where. Had she abandoned him? He didn't understand death. He'd ended up confined in the small apartment and eventually locked up in a metal cage where he could hear the cries of all other cats. Where was he? Simon had joined in the crying himself, but eventually gave up, because no one came to help him.

One visitor had spoken to Simon and asked him "if siamese cats were as mean as they were rumored to be?" To satisfy her curiosity, she'd taken him out of his cage, only to find out that her theory was completely false. Simon had rubbed against her legs and purrred in hopes that she'd adopt him.

He had been at the shelter for over a week when I walked in the door with my neighbor on Tuesday afternoon. A very sad, dejected looking Simon was lying in his cage. My neighbor looked at me and said, "Look how sad his eyes are. He's just given up."

When we asked the kennel attendant for assistance with Simon he replied, "You can get him out yourself. Siamese cats are mean." It was very obvious to us that he was afraid of Simon.

In spite of everything he'd been through, Simon came out of his cage quite willingly. Once in the bonding room, he began to purrr affectionately.

The last thing I'd wanted was another cat, but there was something special about Simon. I decided he was coming home to live with Ophelia and Schnookie. I left him in the bonding area with my neighbor and went to the front desk to fill out adoption papers.

I was in the shelter director's office gathering stories for "Ophelia's Winter" when she instructed the kennel assistant to give Simon a dose of strongid and a 4-in-1 shot.

Since my neighbor was still in the bonding room, I assumed all was well. I later learned that when the kennel assistant had first attempted to administer the strongid to Simon, he went one way and the syringe flew onto the floor. Rejecting my neighbor's offer to help, he had then grabbed Simon, picked up the dirty syringe from the floor and shoved it down his throat.

A phobia about siamese cats is one thing, but cruelty is another. I thanked my lucky stars that I hadn't been there when it happened. Someone besides Simon would have gotten a dose of strongid.

After leaving the shelter with Simon in his carrier, I drove him to my regular vet so he could be checked out and given a rabies shot. Much to my dismay, the vet advised me he was running a fever and had a case of Feline Upper Viral Respiratory Disease. My heart stuck in my throat as I suddenly recalled the tiny sneezes I'd heard at the shelter.

Feline Upper Respiratory Disease is an infection of a cat's upper respiratory tract that involves the nasal cavity and upper airways. The principal source of the infection is from exposure to another cat(s) shedding the virus. A weakness in the immune system, situations of overcrowding, transporting and stress can also be factors contributing to the illness. Simon had become ill for obvious reasons.

The most common sign of F.U.R.D. was the mild to severe sneezing I'd heard in the cat room at the shelter. Viral respiratory disease in cats is extremely contagious. All discharges oral, nasal and ocular are infectious. Contaminated feeding bowls and bedding can transmit the disease from cat to cat. Although not transmittable to human beings, humans can transmit the disease from cat to cat through such procedures as cleaning cages without washing the hands.

Outward signs of the disease include:

(1) Lack of appetite due to blocked nasal passages which inhibits the sense of smell.
(2) Depression and high fever.
(3) Occasionally F.U.R.D. progresses into dehydration, pneumonia and even death.

Before the disease would run its course, Simon would end up fighting a battle for his life. It would take 24-hour care to save him.

At the time of Simon's diagnosis, my options had been to take him home with me as I had originally planned, or drive him back to the shelter and inform them of his condition. The vet didn't even give a thought to the latter choice. She immediately prescribed Clavamox drops for Simon and told me to "keep him isolated from Ophelia and Schnookie for 10 days." She knew me pretty well, because I had no intentions of taking Simon anywhere near the shelter. I was well aware of the fact that he would have been euthanized, had I taken him back there in his condition. Simon deserved better and I was determined he'd have it.

He remained very quiet during the drive home from the vet. Given the extent of his illness, I left him out on the screenporch in the carrier while I prepared his hospital room.

The small downstairs study with wall bookcases and pocket doors proved to be perfect. Simon could sleep on the daybed and enjoy the sunlight from the east and south windows until he recuperated. On warm days, the windows could be raised to air out of the room.

I fixed Simon a litter box with a plastic dish pan, placed a clean, soft pillow on the carpet in front of the daybed, bought in fresh bottled water from the refrigerator and set out some fresh food to see if he would eat.

After turning on the classical music station to low volume, I went back out to the screenporch and carried Simon into his temporary quarters. Miss Ophelia and Schnookie had been very curious as to who was in the carrier, but neither understood why the mysterious stranger was locked up behind closed doors.

I opened the carrier and Simon cautiously made his way out to inspect his new home. He was still affectionate and friendly as he rubbed my legs and purred.

He graciously accepted the food I'd offered and began eating like he hadn't been fed in days. In a matter of minutes, he'd devoured a can of Fancy Feast and gone to the water bowl for a long drink.

It was a warm sunny day, so I opened both windows and Simon got some fresh air. He had jumped up onto the back of the daybed when the professor pulled into his driveway next door. In the blink of an eye, his purring stopped and he stood frozen, glaring at the man. In that same instant, Simon began growling at the professor as though he were going to attack him.

What in the world had happened to the affectionate, sweet cat that had been purring and rubbing my legs only minutes earlier? Was this the norm for a cat who had been an elderly woman's companion for seven years? Were the siamese horror stories really true? Maybe the kennel assistant at the shelter had been justified in his fear of Simon? Maybe I'd made a mistake in adopting him?

After a brief conversation with my neighbor, I knew exactly what was wrong. Simon's abuser had been male, so he'd assumed the professor was the enemy. He had been reacting to the stress of his ordeal just as Miss Ophelia had, but in a different way. The case of Siamese-A-Phobia had been solved.

Per the vet's instructions, I administered the first dose of Clavamox to Simon. I made him comfortable for the evening and decided he needed to get some rest. When I checked on him during the night, he was sound asleep in the middle of his pillow.

By the next morning, Simon's condition had already worsened. His nose was completely blocked and his eyes were showing signs of the infection.

After grabbing an armful of clean towels and washcloths from the closet, I ran a couple of the cloths under the bathroom faucet and very carefully cleaned the end of his nose to remove the obstruction. He looked up at me and seemed to appreciate that he could breathe easier.

In my efforts to protect Schnookie and Miss Ophelia, I immediately threw the washcloths down in the basement with the dirty laundry. I washed my hands thoroughly in the wash basin before I even entered the kitchen.

After feeding Ophelia and Schnookie, I went back into Simon's room and offered him breakfast. He refused food or water and remained on his pillow.

Trying not to be discouraged, but at the same time feeling very concerned, I decided to wait and see if Simon would eat later in the day.

By noon, he had only drank water. At two o'clock, he'd only had water. At three o'clock, only water. Five o'clock rolled around and Simon was still refusing food. He'd also begun sleeping on his pillow, which I figured he needed to do.

As much as I hated to wake him to administer the Clavamox, I also realized that he needed the medication to ward off the infection.

When I went down to check on him during the night, he was once again sound asleep on his pillow.

He'd begun frothing at the mouth by the next morning. I was unable to connect with my regular vet, so I loaded Simon into the carrier and rushed him to the nearest animal hospital where there were qualified professionals.

Simon was quiet during the drive, but once we were in the waiting room, he began to wail and cry in spite of his illness. He heard the sounds of the other cats and dogs in the background and thought I'd taken him back to the shelter. Despite my efforts to comfort him while holding the carrier on my lap, his cries didn't cease.

It was only a few minutes, but it seemed like an eternity before the vet called us into the exam room. I explained to him that I'd adopted Simon from the shelter and his condition had steadily worsened.

Simon frantically resisted the vet's attempts to examine his throat. The doctor finally decided they would have to sedate and keep him overnight. I almost burst into tears.

A very caring staff assured me that Simon would be well taken care of. They could see I was on the verge of crying when I walked out the door.

I broke down when I got to the car. All the way home I kept thinking the same thing. "It wasn't fair. It just wasn't fair. Until a couple weeks ago, Simon had been someone's best friend. Look what happened to him once his owner died. It just wasn't fair."

My heart was pounding when I called to check on him that evening. The vet advised me he was stable and they had administered additional medication. They would provide me with all the details when I picked him up at 9:00 a.m. the next morning.

During my Saturday a.m. conference with the vet, I learned that in addition to U.R.I., Simon had also developed stomatitis, meaning he had inflammatory disease of the mouth. That had explained the frothing.

After the intravenous anesthesia and examination, he had been given a pen/azium injection to further combat both his infections. The vet advised me they were prescribing prednisilone in addition to the antibiotics. Prednisilone is a steroid frequently given to human beings who suffer from asthma.

Once I received all the instructions and the additional medication, my wailing siamese cat was brought out to me in his carrier. His frothing was somewhat but not completely better. He readily recognized me and his cries became louder.

I tried comforting him in hopes that he'd figure out he hadn't been taken back to the shelter. It worked.

By the time I'd gotten him out to the car and opened the door, his cries had almost stopped. In an effort to further calm Simon, I turned on the radio and began singing to him. He became quiet within seconds, because he knew we were headed home again.

Even though I hadn't owned him very long, he seemed to recognize the turn into the driveway. His ears perked up and he raised his head in response to the car's movements.

Once we were back in the study, Simon looked around and began inspecting his room to make certain he was indeed, home again. After a brief glance at me, he curled up onto his pillow to take a long nap. He was happy and contended again. Simon would recover, but he still had a long battle ahead of him.

My chief concern was the fact that Simon still wasn't eating. I'd offered him food up to five times a day and he only drank water. He'd lost a pound in four days.

When he awoke from his nap, I once again tried coaxing him with wet food. He licked some of the gravy, so I was happy.

With an eye dropper in hand, I administered Simon's Clavamox. War was on once he saw me break the prednisilone in half and load it into the pill popper.

Simon proved to be very resistant when it came to his meds. Not to be outdone, I wrapped him up in a fresh bath towel and grabbed the pill popper again. I got the prednisilone down him on the fourth try.

After a ten minute drink of designer water, he was off to his pillow once again. We were both exhausted from the struggle and I was off to bed myself after a hot bath.

I awoke around midnight and tiptoed downstairs to look in on my patient. I wasn't prepared for what I found. Simon had crawled back into the cat carrier and was making very strange sounds. When I heard "Urrrrrrr, Urrrrrrr," I knew he was in trouble.

I quickly threw on a pair of sweats and a shirt, summoned a friend and headed for the emergency clinic with Simon. He vomited in his carrier on the way. The smell was so foul that we had to open the car windows.

When we pulled into the parking lot, I took Simon out of the carrier and threw his towel into a trash bin. After re-lining his carrier with half a roll of paper towels, we rushed him inside.

A young female vet was working the midnight shift, but Simon wasn't going to let anyone look in his mouth. Once again, I gave his medical history. "I had adopted him from the shelter on Tuesday. My regular vet advised me he had Feline Upper Respiratory Disease, was running a fever and would need to be isolated. By Friday, he was frothing at the mouth from stomatitis, in addition to his respiratory infection. He'd been intravenously sedated and hospitalized overnight. It was after midnight on Saturday and he'd taken a sudden turn for the worst."

During Simon's emergency exam, I received further bad news. He was dehydrated. Even though he had been drinking water, he hadn't taken in enough fluids. They would have to administer Sub-Q IV fluids or he wouldn't have a chance.

I nervously waited in the treatment room until a very bloated looking siamese cat was finally brought out to me. Simon looked like they'd blown his sides up with a bicycle pump as I put him back into his carrier.

In addition to the subcutaneous fluids, the vet had also given him a small injection of tagamet to help his nausea. She dispensed half pills of tagamet, along with carafate suspension for further use with Simon.

Due to Simon's stomatitis, or mouth infection, the vet also felt we needed to discontinue the Clavamox drops and use Amoxicillin pills. I was already using the pill popper, so it wouldn't make a lot of difference in the routine.

Simon was almost asleep by the time we left the emergency clinic. I comforted him and told him "what a good boy he was." He looked up at me with his deep blue eyes as though he understood.

When we arrived home again, I sat and watched him sleep for about an hour. Not wanting to waken him from his much needed rest, I left the tiny lamp on in his room and tiptoed down the hall.

The Sub-Q fluids had produced results by the next morning and Simon seemed a little more lively. His breathing was still obstructed by the hardened discharge on his nose, so I once again wet a clean washcloth and gently dabbed his face until he was clean. In spite of the tagamet injection the night before, he still wasn't eating.

I knew I had to get nutrients into his system, so I drove to the local supermarket and purchased several jars of baby food. I was determined to bite the bullet and force feed Simon in spite of his resistance.

An hour later, I had a slightly scratched hand and baby food in my hair. Simon had eaten (via an eyedropper) most of a small jar of turkey n'broth baby food. I'd given him his antibiotic and prednisilone to boot.

While he feel asleep on his pillow to rest up for the next round, I shampooed my hair and changed my clothes. I had never imagined it was going to be so difficult.

The battle of the baby food resumed later that evening and lasted until I'd force fed Simon another six dropperfuls of turkey n'broth. I cleaned him off with a warm, damp washcloth before heading off to bed exhausted from the struggle.

S.O.S.

On Monday morning, I received the scare of my life. While cleaning Simon's nose, I heard another cat sneeze. Pausing just a moment to listen, I realized it was Schnookie. Unbeknownst to me, she had been lurking outside the study door and exposed herself to the virus. I'd been so careful and she'd gotten it anyway.

I burst into tears while I was on the phone with the vet. "Oh God! Not Schnookie, not my baby."

Schnookie and I had been together since she was found on a McDonald's parking lot one cold, damp September evening. She had gone from being a tiny gray feral kitten with ear mites to a working girl in a counseling practice.

In her role as a therapy cat, Schnookie had won hearts and developed countless special relationships with troubled human beings. Clients who had problems seemed to forget their worries when she hopped up onto their laps. I just couldn't picture my life without her, for she had also helped me through many difficult hours.

The vet calmed my fears by reassuring me that "this had indeed, happened more than once. Many healthy cats had let curiosity get the best of them and contracted mild cases of the virus. I was to bring Schnookie in that afternoon and she'd check her out."

Despite the doctor's calm approach, I was still concerned for Schnookie and Miss Ophelia, who was equally special to me. They had both attempted to learn the identity of the mysterious stranger I'd been keeping under wraps. If Schnookie had gotten too close to the door, so had Ophelia.

Schnookie seemed puzzled when I suddenly got her carrier out. She was acting like her cheerful self when we headed for the vet's office.

While we waited in the exam room, I bent down and kissed her on the head. Sensing my panicky mood, she looked up at me as though she were asking, "What's wrong mom?"

The vet found Schnookie's temperature to be normal. She was fine and probably had, at best, "a mild case of the virus." The vet prescribed Clavamox drops for her and Miss Opehlia. I had probably overreacted, but at least I felt better once the vet had examined Schnookie.

Schnookie and I didn't chat with the doctor very long, because I had to get home and take care of Simon. Quite happy to be leaving the vet's office, she sat up in her carrier and observed the speeding traffic. She seemed to know where we were headed when I turned left at the intersection. I could tell she was getting antsy by the time we pulled into the driveway.

Once we were inside the house and I'd opened the carrier door, off she went in a flash. I could have sworn she understood that the vet had given me medicine for her.

Simon was sleeping on his pillow when I went in to check on him. I hated to interrupt his rest, but the amoxicillin and prednisilone had to be administered to him if he were to get well.

Once again we struggled until I finally wrapped him up in a towel. It took five attempts with the pill popper before Simon swallowed his meds.

Next came the eyedropperfuls of baby food, alternated between dropperfuls of designer water. I kept up a steady pace until most of the contents of the small glass jar was either in Simon's stomach or splattered onto both of us.

By the time I'd finished damp wiping his face and fluffing him dry with a clean towel, we were both exhausted. I was more than glad to let him resume his nap and he was happy for me to leave him in peace.

I later administered the Clavamox to Schnookie and Miss Ophelia. Neither were very happy, but they sat and let me put an eyedropper into their mouths. They'd known mom long enough to realize that she knew best and in the end, I always won anyway.

After looking in on Simon for the night, I took a hot bath and fell asleep as soon as my head hit the pillow. It was taking all the energy I had just to pull the little guy through.

While drinking my coffee the next morning, I sat in dread as I contemplated Simon's nose cleaning, feeding and struggling. I finally decided to "get it over with" and opened the pocket doors to the study. Expecting to find him lying on his pillow, I had instead found he was nowhere in sight. For one brief instant, I panicked. Glancing around the room, I spied him curled up asleep inside an adding machine tape box. Just as I had started to lift him out of the box, I had a brainstorm. What if I left him in the box? Maybe it would be easier to administer his meds and feed him?

I lifted Simon, box and all up onto my lap. The pills went down on the first try and he didn't struggle half as much when I fed him. Simon's highchair had been born.

Caring for him suddenly became much easier after my discovery. I even managed to get Soft-Paw nail covers onto his large front paws.

The small cardboard box had been a Godsend. Simon's highchair for sick kitties was my greatest invention.

When Simon jumped up into the screen window on Friday afternoon, I became ecstatic. I was overjoyed at his signs of recovery and told him "what a good boy he was!"

He finally wanted out of the study again on Saturday afternoon. He sat against my leg out on the screenporch, while carefully observing all the comings and goings. It was a beautiful, warm, sunshiny day and being in the fresh air seemed to lift his spirits even more.

He still had a slight cough on Sunday morning and his breath smelled like he'd been on an overnight drunk. It was very obvious he needed further medical attention. I took him back to the clinic for a followup visit, only to encounter another male vet assistant who was afraid of siamese cats.

The young man's siamese-a-phobia became apparent from the moment he opened the door and saw Simon lying on the metal table. His hands trembled as he approached the table to take Simon's temperature and weigh him.

Sensing the man's uneasiness with him, Simon began struggling while the thermometer was in his butt and absolutely refused to have his ears examined. I was holding him on the scale to be weighed when the vet tech asked, "if maybe Simon could be a panic biter?"

Before I even thought about my response, I flew back with a terse, "Absolutely not."

Simon and I had been complete strangers at the time of his adoption. I had done everything to him from washing his face to force feeding and giving him meds with a pill popper. He had never once exhibited any signs of hostility toward me.

Noticing my reaction to him, the vet tech proceeded to explain that as a small child, he'd been attacked by a siamese cat.

In his attempt to escape from the cat, he had tried climbing up onto a well. The cat caught him midway and his legs still bore the scars. Hence, his case of siamese-a-phobia had been more justified than the guy at the shelter. His fear was very real.

We had just finished our discussion when the vet came in. After smelling Simon's breath, he said we needed to administer more antibiotics.

When he lifted the skin on the scruff of his neck, it became apparent that Simon was still somewhat dehydrated. He needed additional Sub-Q fluids.

Simon's weight had dropped from 10 to 8 1/2 pounds, so I would also be force feeding him high maintenance food with extra nutrients for several days. The vet instructed me to mix portions of the food with water to also help re-hydrate Simon.

The struggle with the vet tech began a second time when the vet started Simon's Sub-Q IV bag. He instructed the technician to hold Simon until the bag had emptied. Once again, Simon wanted no part of him. His hands trembled and he began to "overhold" Simon.

For Simon's welfare and that of the vet tech, I politely told him I'd hold onto the cat. The vet returned a few minutes later to find me bent over the table with my cheek pressed against Simon's face while comforting him. The vet tech was standing against the wall observing as the IV flowed smoothly.

As we waited for the IV bag to finish emptying, the vet told us a cat story. "Early on in his career, he had been called in to care for a cat that wouldn't eat. This particular cat had been the companion of an elderly woman and remained on the foot of her bed until her death. The cat's grief was so intense, that it never ate another bite."

When I was leaving the clinic with Simon, the vet looked me in the eye and left me with a parting thought. "No good deed goes unrewarded. Take good care of my cat."

Early Monday morning, Simon's litter pan was full of pee. He was sitting in the middle of the floor grooming himself for the first time since he'd been adopted from the shelter.

Two problems still remained. His nose was clogged again and he wasn't eating on his own.

Happy about the fact that he was grooming himself and unhappy that he still wasn't eating, I cleaned his nose off with a warm, wet washcloth.

As usual, he exhibited some displeasure when I put him into "Simey's highchair" to begin my routine of medicating and force feeding him. I readily noticed he'd regained some of his strength.

Once I'd cleaned the splattered cat food out of his coat and my face, Simon jumped up onto the window sill. Instead of going back to sleep, he'd decided to watch the squirrels outside.

Simon's spirits had remained high on Tuesday and I offered him some food in a bowl. He licked most of the gravy and swallowed a little of the food in the process. I knew he wouldn't be happy, but I put him back into his highchair once again for medication and force feeding. I'd become determined we weren't going to loose any ground in his recovery process.

When I looked in on him before bedtime, I left half a can of food in a dish beside his water bowl. I kept my fingers crossed, because I knew that his eating even a spoonful on his own would be a major breakthrough.

My prayers were finally answered. Whenever I went downstairs on Wednesday morning, Simon had eaten most of the food in his bowl and was crying for more. His siamese "Waaaa's" were music to my ears. I sat watching in amazement as he consumed bite after bite of nutritious food.

After I'd given him his meds with the pill popper, he wanted to go out onto the screenporch for some fresh air. I stood in the door crying as Simon sat in the warm morning sun watching the birds and squirrels. He had survived.

Simon was beating on the pocket doors and wailing at 3:00 a.m. the next morning. He'd once again decided that he wanted out of the study. This time, he wanted to explore his new home and meet his two sisters.

He ended up lying side by side with Schnookie on the screenporch and sharing toys with Miss Ophelia. He was indeed, a handsome, well-trained gentleman.

Amidst all the confusion, it hadn't dawned on me that after Simon's adoption, the initials of my three cats translated to

118

S.O.S. or Schnookie, Ophelia and Simon. I truly had been meant to be his new mom, to care for and love him.

Through more than one firsthand experience, I have been made aware that the majority of people, including the wealthy, do not plan for their pets. As much as I would like to, I could rent a U-haul truck and back it up to the door of the animal shelter tomorrow. The problem of abandoned companion animals wouldn't go away, because there would be more of them arriving at the shelter the next day and the next.

WHEN THERE'S A WILL THERE'S A WAY

Singer Dusty Springfield was an icon in the music industry. Her first hit record was in 1964, when she recorded "I Only Want To Be With You."

Dusty was initially diagnosed with breast cancer in 1994. She underwent chemotherapy for a year and was given a clean bill of health. Her cancer recurred by the following year.

Many people assumed that Dusty feared her impending death, but it wasn't death itself that became foremost in her mind. Dusty Springfield worried about what would become of Nicholas, her soul mate of 13 years. Nicholas was a California Rag-Doll cat she'd bought when on a trip.

She knew she didn't have the strength to fight the disease that was ravaging her body, so she became determined to make sure Nicholas didn't suffer after she was gone. Dusty willed Nicholas to one of her best friends, faith healer Lee Everett-Alkin. Like Dusty, Lee was also an animal lover. She and her husband John Alkin made sure that Nicholas received the best of care.

They didn't want Nicholas to ever forget his mistress. After Dusty's death, he slept on a pillow from her bed and snuggled up in the nightgown she wore when she passed away at her home.

Shortly before her death, Dusty had made arrangements for a year's supply of canned baby food to be shipped from the United States for Nicholas. Lee and John made sure that Nicholas had the food Dusty ordered for him. They also made sure that Dusty's tapes were played for Nicholas during his catnaps so he would be comforted by her voice.

Dusty had bought Nicholas a 7 foot high indoor tree house studded with hearts when they'd lived in Holland. The wooden house, along with its garden of foilage and carpeted apartments was also willed to Lee Alkin. It was moved into her bungalow in Berkshire, England.

Lee and her husband added on an 8 foot extension to their house for Nicholas. Inside the bungalow, a wire-mesh grill temporarily separated Nicholas from Lee's cat Purrdie and her dogs. She and Dusty had always felt the two cats should be together. Lee had arranged a "marriage" for them even though they were both spayed/neutered.

At the time of Dusty's death, she and Lee had been friends for 30 years. Lee was happy that she could lay her friend's mind to rest about what would happen to Nicholas.

Although the treatment of Nicholas may seem eccentric to many people, all pet lovers, American and European love their companions. The English are much more humane and of course, most pet owners do not have the financial resources of Dusty Springfield.

In spite of the monetary differences and English vs United States Law Codes, Dusty Springfield's bequest had followed some fundamental guidelines. Dusty had used her last will and testament to confirm the transfer of Nicholas to Lee Alkin, who had made a commitment to providing alternative care to her pet cat. She and Dusty had a prior understanding of how he would be cared for. Dusty had made it clear that legal custody of Nicholas had already been transferred to Lee Alkin by their mutual understanding, so that the matter of transferring Nicholas to Lee didn't become just another item that needed to go through court proceedings. Their solution had required a high degree of trust, but Dusty and Lee had been friends for 30 years at the time Dusty died.

While she was still well enough and competent to do so, Dusty Springfield had lined up a friend whose personality and circumstances were compatible with her cat Nicholas. Lee was also an animal lover who owned a cat and two dogs. She'd been willing to make a commitment to take care of Nicholas for the rest of his natural life after Dusty's death.

Dusty just hadn't left Nicholas to Lee without talking to her and feeling comfortable about her decision. She and Dusty had always felt that Purrdie and Nicholas should be together. Lee Alkin was quite aware of what was involved and more than willing to accept Nicholas.

Each of us who has pets and is concerned about what will happen to them when we die must face the fact that we have a very predictable problem. It must be addressed during our lifetime, if it is to be resolved in any meaningful and satisfactory manner.

Right now, decide who will care for your pet(s) if you should become ill or die. Make sure they are willing and able to do it. Talk to them. If you are planning to have an organization care for your cat or dog, or arrange for its placement, check them out first. Confirm any advance arrangements they need. If you want to use your will or create a trust for your animal(s), don't try doing it yourself. This is a tricky area for skilled lawyers. For an unskilled person, such an effort would almost certainly fail. Keep in mind that, "the more money involved, the more likely your relatives will be to challenge it in court." Make sure others know about your companion animal and that you have already made arrangements for their care and disposition. If something should happen to you, your pet needs care and attention immediately.

There are scores of cases which almost invariably have a tragic ending. These cases have arisen solely because the person(s) involved did not attend to this very critical matter during his/her lifetime.

BIBLIOGRAPHY

Arena, Salvatore, The New York Daily News, "Testament to Family JFK Jr. leaves sis, kids his estate", New York, September 25, 1999.

Armstrong, Martha C., "ABC/HSUS CAMPAIGN-CATS INDOORS", September, 1997.

AANA News Bulletins, "Biography Janet E. McMahon, Volume Numbers 9-#3, August, 1939, 9-#3, August ,1941, 8-#4, October, 1954, 9-#2, April, 155, 30-#4, July, 1976," Park Ridge, Illinois.

American Psychiatric Association, "Diagnostic and Statistical Manual of Mental Disorders," Washington, D.C., 1994.

Animal Protection Association, "Pet Theft", Memphis, Tennessee, September, 1998.

Animal Legal Defense Fund, "The Link Between Animal Abuse and Human Violence." Petaluma, California, 1999.

American Society for the Prevention of Cruelty to Animals, "Animal Watch", Volume 18, No. 4, New York, Winter, 1998.

ASPCA Companion Animal Services, "Bringing in a Second Cat", "The Isolation Area", New York, N.Y., 1999.

Bolster, Larry, "Why We Shouldn't Tolerate Animal Cruelty.", Maine, May, 1998.

Cooper, Geoffrey M., "Elements of Human Cancer", Bartlett Publishers: Boston, Massachusetts, 1992.

Fox, Claire, "Upper Respiratory Infections/Feline Medicine", TICA Outstanding Cattery, June 3, 1997, 1995.

Harpham, Wendy Schlessel, M.D., " Diagnosis Cancer, Your Guide Through The First Few Months," W.W. Norton & Company, New York, 1992.

Kaplan, Melissa, "Ball Pythons", 1996.

Madden, Murdaugh Steward and Roger Kindler, "Law Notes: Planning For The Future, The Humane Society of the United States News," Washington, D.C., Fall, 1989.

McElroy, Susan Chernak, "Animals As Teachers and Healers". NewSage Press Troutdale, Oregon, 1996.

McGonagle, John J. Jr., "Planning For Your Cat's Care--If You Are No Longer There", "CATS Magazine, Peoria, Illinois, September, 1992.

Perry, Tina, "Adopting from a Shelter", Animal Protection Institute of America, Sacramento, California.

Mersol, Mary Jo Barg & Joan Miller, "CFA Breed Profiles", Cat Fancier's Association, Manasquan, New Jersey, 1995.

Richardson, Angela Hunter, "Stress and the Cat You Love", CatLife, Ft. Worth, Texas, 1997-98.

Saltonstall, Dave, The New York Daily News, "Dog Friday, Cat Ruby Safe", New York, July 25, 1999.

Schwartz, Dr. Stephanie, "Training Your Child To Be 'Pet Wise," Boston Massachusetts, 1998.

Senior's Site, "The Healing Power of Pets", Boca Raton, Florida, 1996.

Smith, H. Allen, "RHUBARB", Doubleday & Company, Inc., The Country Life Press, Garden City, New York, 1946.

The Sunday Mirror, "Dusty Springfield", April 4, 1999, Mirror Group, Canary Wharf, London, England, E145AP.

United States Department of Agriculture--Animal & Plant Health Inspection Service, "Safeguarding Pets", Riverdale, Maryland, September, 1997.

About the Author

One of the most famous historical events in Appalachia was the "Miner's March" and confrontation with federal troops which took place at Lens Creek. This event was depicted in the movie "MATEWAN". I was born on Sunday, October, 17, 1948 in Charleston, West Virginia and grew up on Lens Creek, three miles from where the famous confrontation took place.

My pseudonym, Sarah Ann Hill, was my great-grandmother's name. She was a family storyteller back in the 1800's.

Since my great-grandfather was West Virginia's first forest ranger, I come by my love for animals naturally. He was a kind, gentle man with soft blue eyes who never met a stranger. He lived until the early 1960's, so I was fortunate enough to have known him.

After my high school graduation at age seventeen, I moved to Washington, D.C., where I worked as a federal employee for a brief period of time. I returned to West Virginia, where I spent the next eight years working for Charleston Newspapers, Inc. In addition to being a senior accounting clerk, I also did my first technical and general writing while training people. I was exposed to reporters on a daily basis. During this time, I earned A.S. and B.S. degrees in Accounting from Morris Harvey College/The University of Charleston.

I have spent twenty plus years in the field of Accounting as a manager/cost accountant, tax accountant, etc., having worked for both Fortune 250 and Fortune 500 companies. My accounting jobs have not only given me extensive experience in technical and general writing, but much travel experience throughout the United States. I also have presentation and teaching experience from my corporate background(s).

I've never considered myself an activist, but the more I learned about Ophelia and Miss Janet, the angrier I became. All life is a divine gift and cruelty should not be tolerated in any form.